56th Annual Meeting of the Association for Computational Linguistics (ACL 2018)

Tutorial Abstracts

Melbourne, Australia
15 – 20 July 2018

ISBN: 978-1-5108-6709-3

Printed from e-media with permission by:

Curran Associates, Inc.
57 Morehouse Lane
Red Hook, NY 12571

Some format issues inherent in the e-media version may also appear in this print version.

Printed by Curran Associates, Inc. (2018)

For permission requests, please contact the Association for Computational Linguistics at the address below.

Association for Computational Linguistics
209 N. Eighth Street
Stroudsburg, Pennsylvania 18360

Phone: 1-570-476-8006
Fax: 1-570-476-0860

acl@aclweb.org

Additional copies of this publication are available from:

Curran Associates, Inc.
57 Morehouse Lane
Red Hook, NY 12571 USA
Phone: 845-758-0400
Fax: 845-758-2633
Email: curran@proceedings.com
Web: www.proceedings.com

ACL 2018

The 56th Annual Meeting of the Association for Computational Linguistics

Proceedings of the Conference Tutorial Abstracts

July 15 - 20, 2018
Melbourne, Australia

Message from the Tutorial Chairs

This volume contains the abstracts of the ACL 2018 tutorials. Tutorials were selected from 49 submissions to a joint call, which was coordinated with NAACL, COLING, and EMNLP. From these submissions, eight half-day tutorials were selected for ACL, on the criteria of quality, relevance, interest, and balance. We thank Mausam for coordinating this process across all four conferences, and we wish to acknowledge support from the publications chairs Kevin Gimpel, Shay Cohen, and Wei Lu (ACL publications chairs) and Jey Han Lau and Trevor Cohn (ACL handbook chairs), as well as Stephanie Lukin (NAACL publications co-chair). Most importantly, we thank the tutorial presenters for their contributions, which we hope that you will enjoy.

ACL 2018 Tutorial Chairs
Yoav Artzi, Cornell University
Jacob Eisenstein, Georgia Institute of Technology

Tutorial Chairs:

Yoav Artzi, Cornell University
Jacob Eisenstein, Georgia Institute of Technology

Table of Contents

Conference Program

Sunday, July 15, 2018

09:00–12:30

100 Things You Always Wanted to Know about Semantics & Pragmatics But Were Afraid to Ask
Emily M. Bender

09:00–12:30

Neural Approaches to Conversational AI
Jianfeng Gao, Michel Galley and Lihong Li

09:00–12:30

Variational Inference and Deep Generative Models
Wilker Aziz and Philip Schulz

09:00–12:30

Connecting Language and Vision to Actions
Peter Anderson, Abhishek Das and Qi Wu

Sunday, July 15, 2018 (continued)

13:30–17:00

Beyond Multiword Expressions: Processing Idioms and Metaphors
Valia Kordoni

13:30–17:00

Neural Semantic Parsing
Matt Gardner, Pradeep Dasigi, Srinivasan Iyer, Alane Suhr and Luke Zettlemoyer

13:30–17:00

Deep Reinforcement Learning for NLP
William Yang Wang, Jiwei Li and Xiaodong He

13:30–17:00

Multi-lingual Entity Discovery and Linking
Avi Sil, Heng Ji, Dan Roth and Silviu-Petru Cucerzan

100 Things You Always Wanted to Know about Semantics & Pragmatics But Were Afraid to Ask*

Emily M. Bender
University of Washington
Department of Linguistics
Box 3542425
Seattle WA 98195-2425 USA
ebender@uw.edu

1 Tutorial overview

Meaning is a fundamental concept in Natural Language Processing (NLP), given its aim to build systems that mean what they say to you, and understand what you say to them. In order for NLP to scale beyond partial, task-specific solutions, it must be informed by what is known about how humans use language to express and understand communicative intents. The purpose of this tutorial is to present a selection of useful information about semantics and pragmatics, as understood in linguistics, in a way that's accessible to and useful for NLP practitioners with minimal (or even no) prior training in linguistics.

The tutorial will look at both aspects of meaning tied to the linguistic signal (sentence meaning), including how it is tied to syntactic structure, and aspects of meaning in situated language use (speaker meaning). For the most part, the points will be illustrated with English examples, but to the extent possible I will bring in a typological perspective to foster an understanding of to what extent phenomena are crosslinguistically variable and to highlight semantic phenomena that are not present in English.

The tutorial will briefly cover the following six topics:

1. Introduction: What is meaning? What is the difference between speaker meaning and sentence meaning? How do they relate to the tasks of interest to participants?

2. Lexical semantics: What do words mean? What kind of formally precise devices allow for compact representations and tractable inference with word meanings? How are those meanings related to each other? How do those meanings change over time?

3. Semantics of phrases: How do we build the meaning of the phrase from the meaning of the parts? How should one tackle (possibly partially) non-compositional elements like multi-word expressions?

4. Meaning beyond the sentence: How do sentences in discourse relate to each other? How do we connect referring expressions with the same referents?

5. Presupposition and implicature: What are presuppositions and implicatures? What linguistic expressions introduce presuppositions and how do they interact in larger structures? How do we calculate implicatures?

6. Resources: What linguistic resources have been built to assist with semantic processing?

2 Instructor

Emily M. Bender is a Professor in the Department of Linguistics and Adjunct Professor in the Paul G. Allen School of Computer Science & Engineering at the University of Washington. She is also the past chair (2016–2017) of NAACL. Her research interests lie in multilingual grammar engineering, computational semantics, and the incorporation of linguistic knowledge in natural language processing. She is the PI of the Grammar Matrix grammar customization system, which is developed in the context of the DELPH-IN Consortium (Deep Linguistic Processing with HPSG Initiative). More generally, she is interested in the intersection of linguistics and computational linguistics, from both directions: bringing computational methodologies to linguistic science and linguistic science to natural language processing.

*. . . for fear of being told 1000 more

Proceedings of the 56th Annual Meeting of the Association for Computational Linguistics-Tutorial Abstracts, page 1
Melbourne, Australia, July 15 - 20, 2018.

Neural Approaches to Conversational AI

Jianfeng Gao
Microsoft AI & Research
Redmond, WA, USA
jfgao@microsoft.com

Michel Galley
Microsoft AI & Research
Redmond, WA, USA
mgalley@acm.org

Lihong Li
Google Inc.
Kirkland, WA, USA
lihong@google.com

Abstract

This tutorial surveys neural approaches to conversational AI that were developed in the last few years. We group conversational systems into three categories: (1) question answering agents, (2) task-oriented dialogue agents, and (3) social bots. For each category, we present a review of state-of-the-art neural approaches, draw the connection between neural approaches and traditional symbolic approaches, and discuss the progress we have made and challenges we are facing, using specific systems and models as case studies.

1 Motivation and objectives

Developing an intelligent dialogue system that not only emulates human conversation, but also can answer questions of topics ranging from latest news of a movie star to Einstein's theory of relativity, and fulfill complex tasks such as travel planning, has been one of the longest running goals in AI. The goal remains elusive until recently when we started observing promising results in both the research community and industry as the large amount of conversation data is available for training and the breakthroughs in deep learning (DL) and reinforcement learning (RL) are applied to conversational AI.

This tutorial presents a review of state of the art neural approaches to conversational AI that were developed in the last few years, draws the connection between neural approaches and traditional symbolic approaches, and discusses the progress we have made and challenges we are facing, using specific systems and models as case studies.

This tutorial is a valuable resource for students, researchers, and the software developers, providing a detailed presentation of the important ideas and insights needed to understand and create modern dialogue agents that are instrumental to making the world knowledge and services accessible to millions of users in the most natural way.

2 The tutorial

In this tutorial, we start with a brief introduction to the recent progress on DL and RL that is related to natural language processing (NLP), information retrieval (IR) and conversational AI. Then, we describe in detail the state-of-the-art neural approaches developed for three types of dialogue systems. The first is a question answering (QA) agent. Equipped with rich knowledge drawn from various data sources including Web documents and pre-complied knowledge graphs (KG's), the QA agent can provide concise direct answers to user queries. The second is a task-oriented dialogue system that can help users accomplish tasks ranging from meeting scheduling to vacation planning. The third is a social chat bot which can converse seamlessly and appropriately with humans, and often plays roles of a chat companion and a recommender. In the final part of the tutorial, we review attempts to developing open-domain conversational AI systems that combine the strengths of different types of dialogue systems.

2.1 A Unified View: Dialogue as Optimal Decision Making

The example dialogue presented in Table 1 can be formulated as a sequential decision making process. It has a natural hierarchy: a top-level process selects what agent to activate for a particular subtask (e.g., answer a question, schedule a meeting, give a recommendation or just have a chat etc.), and a low level process, perform by the selected agent, chooses primitive actions to complete the subtask.

Proceedings of the 56th Annual Meeting of the Association for Computational Linguistics-Tutorial Abstracts, pages 2–7
Melbourne, Australia, July 15 - 20, 2018.

usr:	Where are sales lagging behind our forecast?
agt:	The worst region is [country], where sales are 15% below projections.
usr:	Do you know why?
agt:	The forecast for [product] growth was overly optimistic.
usr:	How can we turn this around?
agt:	Here are the 10 customers in [country] with the most growth potential, per our CRM model.
usr:	Can you set up a meeting with the CTO of [company]?
agt:	Yes, I've set up a meeting with [person name] for next month when you are in [location].
usr:	Thanks.

Table 1: A human-agent dialogue during a process of making a business decision. (*usr*: user, *agt*: agent)

Such hierarchical decision making processes can be formulated in the mathematical framework of *options over Markov Decision Processes (MDPs)* (Sutton et al., 1999), where options generalize primitive actions to higher-level actions. This is an extension to the traditional MDP setting where an agent can only choose a primitive action at each time step, with options the agent can choose a multi-step action which for example could be a sequence of primitive actions for completing a subtask.

If we view each option as an action, both top-level and low-level processes can be naturally mapped to the reinforcement learning (RL) framework as follows. The dialogue agent navigates a MDP, interacting with its environment over a sequence of discrete steps. At step, the agent observes the current state, and chooses an action a according to a policy. The agent then receives reward and observe a new state, continuing the cycle until the episode terminates. The goal of dialogue learning is to find optimal policies to maximize expected rewards. Table 2 summarizes all dialogue agents using a unified view of RL.

Although RL provides a unified machine learning (ML) framework for building dialogue agents, applying RL requires training a dialogue agent by interacting with real users, which can be very expensive for many domains. Thus, in practice we often use RL together with supervised learning especially in the cases where there is a large amount of human-human conversational data. In the rest of the tutorial, we will survey these ML approaches.

2.2 Question Answering and Machine Reading Comprehension

Recent years have witnessed an increasing demand for question answering (QA) dialogue agents that allow users to query large scale knowledge bases (KB) or document collections via natural language. The former is known as KB-QA agents and the latter text-QA agents. KB-QA agents are superior to traditional SQL-like systems in that users can query a KB interactively without composing complicated SQL-like queries. Text-QA agents are superior to traditional search engines, such as Bing and Google, in that they provide concise direct answers to user queries.

In this part, we start with a review of traditional symbolic approaches to KB-QA based on semantic parsing. We show that a symbolic system is hard to scale because the keyword-matching-based inference used by the system is inefficient for a big KB, and is not robust to paraphrasing. To address these issues, neural approaches are developed to represent queries and KB using continuous semantic vectors so that the inference can be performed at the semantic level in a compacted neural space. We use ReasoNet with shared memory (Shen et al., 2017) as an example to illustrate the implementation details. We also review different dialogue policies for multi-turn KB-QA agents.

We then discuss neural text-QA agents. The heart of such systems is a neural Machine Reading Comprehension (MRC) model that generates an answer to an input query based on a set of passages. After reviewing popular MRC datasets, we describe the technologies developed for state-of-the-art MRC models in two dimensions: (1) the methods of encoding query and passages as vectors in a neural space, and (2) the methods of performing inference in the neural space to generate the answer.

We end this section by outlining our effort of turning Microsoft Bing from a Web search engine into an open-domain QA engine.

2.3 Task-Oriented Dialogue Systems

In this part, we first introduce the architecture of a typical task-oriented dialogue system. It consists of (1) a natural language understanding (NLU)

dialogue	state	action	reward
QA	understanding of user query intent	clarification questions or answers	relevance of answer # of dialogue turns
task-oriented	understanding of user goal	dialogue-act and slot/value	task success rate # of dialogue turns
chatbot	conversation history and user intent	response	user engagement
top-level bot	understanding of user top-level intent	options	daily/monthly usage

Table 2: Reinforcement Learning for Dialogue.

module for identifying intents of user utterances; (2) a state tracker for tracking conversation state; (3) a dialogue policy which selects the next action based on the current state; and (4) a natural language generator (NLG) for converting the agent action to a natural language response. While traditionally these modules are often implemented and optimized individually using statistical models and/or hand-craft rules (Young et al., 2013; Tur and De Mori, 2011), there is a growing interest in applying deep learning and reinforcement learning to automate the optimization of a dialogue system.

We describe state-of-the-art approaches in two frontiers. The first is end-to-end (E2E) learning where these modules are implemented using differentiable models like neural networks, so that they can be jointly optimized from user feedback signals using backpropagation and RL. The second is the use of advanced RL techniques to optimize dialogue policies in more complex scenarios. Examples include improved efficiency of exploration for faster learning, and hierarchical problem solving for composite-task dialogues where the reward signal is particularly sparse. We review several recent proposals, including the ones based on Bayesian models, curiosity-driven strategy, hierarchical reinforcement learning, adversarial learning, and the Dyna framework (Sutton, 1990; Peng et al., 2018) to integrate planning and learning, etc.

We end this section by presenting a few example task-oriented systems from some of the leading players in the industry, including Microsoft's Cortana, Amazon's Alexa and Google's Assistant.

2.4 Fully Data-Driven Conversation Models and Social Bots

Social bots (also known as chatbots) are of growing importance in facilitating smooth interaction between humans and their electronic devices. Recently, researchers have begun to explore fully data-driven generation of conversational responses within the framework of neural machine translation (NMT) in the form of encoder-decoder or seq2seq models (Sordoni et al., 2015; Vinyals and Le, 2015; Serban et al., 2016). Such end-to-end models have been particularly successful with social bot scenarios, as they require little interaction with the user's environment (no need for API calls) and such models cope well with free-form and open domain texts.

However, neural responses are often too general to carry meaningful information, e.g., with the common response "I don't know" which can serve as a reply to most user questions. A mutual information model is proposed by (Li et al., 2016a), and is later improved by using deep reinforcement learning (Li et al., 2016c). Furthermore, Li et al.(Li et al., 2016b) presented a persona-based model to address the issue of speaker consistency in neural response generation.

Although task-oriented dialogue systems and social bots are originally developed for different purposes, there is a trend of combining both as a step towards building an open-domain dialogue agent. For example, on the one hand, (Ghazvininejad et al., 2018) presented a fully data-driven and knowledge-grounded neural conversation model aimed at producing more contentful responses without slot filling. On the other hand, Zhao et al. (Zhao et al., 2017) proposed a task-oriented dialogue agent based on the encoder-decoder model with chatting capability. These works represent steps toward end-to-end dialogue systems that are useful in scenarios beyond chitchat.

We end this section by presenting a few examples of chatbots that have been made available to the public, including Microsoft's XiaoIce, Replika and Alexa Prize systems.

3 Contributions and related tutorials

Conversational AI, which aims to develop intelligent agents for QA, social chat and task-completion, as presented in this tutorial, is a rapidly growing field. Recently, there have been related tutorial and survey papers on deep learning and dialogue systems. (Yih et al., 2015, 2016; Gao, 2017) reviewed deep learning approaches to a wide range of NLP and IR tasks, including dialogue. (Chen et al., 2017b) is a recent tutorial on dialogue mainly focusing on task-oriented agents. (Serban et al., 2015) gave a good survey of public dialogue datasets that can used to develop dialogue agents. (Chen et al., 2017a) reviewed popular deep neural network models for dialogue, focusing only on supervised learning approaches. This tutorial expands the scope of (Chen et al., 2017a) and (Serban et al., 2015) by going beyond data and supervised learning.

The contributions of this tutorial include:

1. We provide a comprehensive survey on neural approaches to conversational AI that were developed in the last few years, covering QA, task-oriented and social bots with a unified view of optimal decision making.

2. We draw connections between modern neural approaches and traditional symbolic approaches, allowing us to better understand why and how the research has been evolved and shed light on how we move forward.

3. We present state-of-the-art approaches to training dialogue agents using both supervised learning and reinforcement learning methods.

4. We picture the landscape of conversational systems developed in research communities and released in industry, demonstrating via case studies the progress we have made and the challenges we are facing.

4 Format and detailed schedule

The tutorial consists of four parts. The detailed schedule is as follows.

1. Part 1 (15 minutes): Introduction
    - Who should attend this tutorial?
    - Dialogue: what kinds of problem?
    - A unified view: dialogue as optimal decision making
    - Machine learning basics
    - Deep learning leads to paradigm shift in NLP
    - Reinforcement learning

2. Part 2 (45 minutes): QA and MRC
    - The KB-QA task
    - Semantic parsing
    - Embedding-based KB-QA
    - Multi-turn KB-QA agents
    - Machine reading for Text-QA
    - Neural MRC models
    - QA in Bing

3. Part 3 (50 minutes): Task-oriented dialogue
    - Overview and architecture
    - Review of traditional approaches
    - Natural language understanding and dialogue state tracking
    - Evaluation and user simulator
    - Neural approaches and E2E learning
    - RL for dialogue policy learning
    - Task-oriented bots in industry

4. Part 4 (50 minutes): Fully data-driven conversation models and chatbots
    - E2E neural conversation models, e.g., seq2seq, HRED, etc.
    - Challenges and remedies
    - Grounded conversation models
    - Beyond supervised learning
    - Data and evaluation
    - Chatbots in public
    - Future work: toward more goal-oriented E2E conversational systems

5 About the presenters

Jianfeng Gao is Partner Research Manager at Microsoft AI and Research, Redmond. He leads the development of AI systems for machine reading comprehension, question answering, chitchat bots, task-oriented dialogue, and business applications. From 2014 to 2017, he was Partner Research Manager and Principal Researcher at Deep Learning Technology Center at Microsoft Research, Redmond, where he was leading the research on deep learning for text and image processing. From 2006 to 2014, he was Researcher, Senior Researcher, and Principal Researcher at Natural Language Processing Group at Microsoft Research, Redmond, where he worked on the Bing search engine, improving its core relevance engine and query spelling, understanding and reformulation engines, MS ads relevance and prediction, and statistical machine translation. From 2005 to 2006, he was a Research Lead in Natural Interactive Services Division at Microsoft, where he worked on Project X, an effort of developing natural user interface for Windows. From 2000 to 2005, he was Research Lead in Natural Language Computing Group at Microsoft Research Asia, where he and his colleagues developed the first Chinese speech recognition system released with Microsoft Office, the Chinese/Japanese Input Method Editors (IME) which were the leading products in the market, and the natural language platform for Microsoft Windows.

Michel Galley is a Senior Researcher at Microsoft Research. His research interests are in the areas of natural language processing and machine learning, with a particular focus on conversational AI, text generation, and machine translation. From 2007 to 2010, he was a Postdoctoral Scholar then Research Associate in the Computer Science department at Stanford University, working primarily on Machine Translation. In 2007, he obtained his Ph.D. from the Computer Science department at Columbia University, with research focusing on summarization, discourse, and dialogue. From 2003 to 2005, he did several internships at USC/ISI and Language Weaver on machine translation, which included work that won several NIST MT competitions. From 2000-2001, he did an 8-month internship and undergraduate thesis work in the Spoken Dialog Systems group at Bell Labs, working on generation for dialogue systems.

Lihong Li is a Research Scientist at Google Inc. He obtained a PhD degree in Computer Science from Rutgers University, specializing in reinforcement learning theory and algorithms. After that, he has held Researcher, Senior Researcher, and Principal Researcher positions in Yahoo! Research (2009-2012) and Microsoft Research (2012-2017), before joining Google. His main research interests are reinforcement learning (in both Markov decision processes and contextual bandits) and other related problems in AI (including active leaning, online learning and large-scale machine learning). His work has found applications in recommendation, advertising, Web search and conversation systems, and has won best paper awards at ICML, AISTATS and WSDM. In recent years, he served as area chairs or senior program committee members at AAAI, AISTATS, ICML, IJCAI and NIPS. More information can be found on his homepage: http://lihongli.github.io .

References

Hongshen Chen, Xiaorui Liu, Dawei Yin, and Jiliang Tang. 2017a. A survey on dialogue systems: Recent advances and new frontiers. *arXiv preprint arXiv:1711.01731*.

Yun-Nung Chen, Asli Celikyilmaz, and Dilek Hakkani-Tür. 2017b. Deep learning for dialogue systems. *Proceedings of ACL 2017, Tutorial Abstracts*, pages 8–14.

Jianfeng Gao. 2017. An introduction to deep learning for natural language processing. In *International Summer School on Deep Learning, Bilbao*.

Marjan Ghazvininejad, Chris Brockett, Ming-Wei Chang, Bill Dolan, Jianfeng Gao, Wen-tau Yih, and Michel Galley. 2018. A knowledge-grounded neural conversation model. In *AAAI*.

Jiwei Li, Michel Galley, Chris Brockett, Jianfeng Gao, and Bill Dolan. 2016a. A diversity-promoting objective function for neural conversation models. In *NAACL-HLT*.

Jiwei Li, Michel Galley, Chris Brockett, Jianfeng Gao, and Bill Dolan. 2016b. A persona-based neural conversation model. In *ACL*.

Jiwei Li, Will Monroe, Alan Ritter, Dan Jurafsky, Michel Galley, and Jianfeng Gao. 2016c. Deep reinforcement learning for dialogue generation. In *EMNLP*.

Baolin Peng, Xiujun Li, Jianfeng Gao, Jingjing Liu, and Kam-Fai Wong. 2018. Integrating planning for task-completion dialogue policy learning. *arXiv preprint arXiv:1801.06176*.

Iulian Vlad Serban, Ryan Lowe, Peter Henderson, Laurent Charlin, and Joelle Pineau. 2015. A survey of available corpora for building data-driven dialogue systems. *arXiv preprint arXiv:1512.05742*.

Iulian Vlad Serban, Alessandro Sordoni, Yoshua Bengio, Aaron C Courville, and Joelle Pineau. 2016. Building end-to-end dialogue systems using generative hierarchical neural network models. In *AAAI*, pages 3776–3784.

Yelong Shen, Po-Sen Huang, Ming-Wei Chang, and Jianfeng Gao. 2017. Traversing knowledge graph in vector space without symbolic space guidance. *arXiv preprint arXiv:1611.04642*.

Alessandro Sordoni, Michel Galley, Michael Auli, Chris Brockett, Yangfeng Ji, Margaret Mitchell, Jian-Yun Nie, Jianfeng Gao, and Bill Dolan. 2015. A neural network approach to context-sensitive generation of conversational responses. In *NAACL-HLT*.

Richard S Sutton. 1990. Integrated architectures for learning, planning, and reacting based on approximating dynamic programming. In *Proceedings of the seventh international conference on machine learning*, pages 216–224.

Richard S. Sutton, Doina Precup, and Satinder P. Singh. 1999. Between MDPs and semi-MDPs: A framework for temporal abstraction in reinforcement learning. *Artificial Intelligence*, 112(1–2):181–211. An earlier version appeared as Technical Report 98-74, Department of Computer Science, University of Massachusetts, Amherst, MA 01003. April, 1998.

Gokhan Tur and Renato De Mori. 2011. *Spoken language understanding: Systems for extracting semantic information from speech*. John Wiley & Sons.

Oriol Vinyals and Quoc Le. 2015. A neural conversational model. In *ICML Deep Learning Workshop*.

Wen-tau Yih, Xiaodong He, and Jianfeng Gao. 2015. Deep learning and continuous representations for natural language processing. In *Proceedings of the 2015 Conference of the North American Chapter of the Association for Computational Linguistics: Tutorial*.

Wen-tau Yih, Xiaodong He, and Jianfeng Gao. 2016. Deep learning and continuous representations for natural language processing. In *IJCAI: Tutorial*.

Steve Young, Milica Gašić, Blaise Thomson, and Jason D Williams. 2013. Pomdp-based statistical spoken dialog systems: A review. *Proceedings of the IEEE*, 101(5):1160–1179.

Tiancheng Zhao, Allen Lu, Kyusong Lee, and Maxine Eskenazi. 2017. Generative encoder-decoder models for task-oriented spoken dialog systems with chatting capability. *arXiv preprint arXiv:1706.08476*.

Variational Inference and Deep Generative Models

Wilker Aziz
ILLC
University of Amsterdam
w.aziz@uva.nl

Philip Schulz
Amazon Research
phschulz@amazon.com

1 Tutorial Contents

Neural networks are taking NLP by storm. Yet they are mostly applied to fully supervised tasks. Many real-world NLP problems require unsupervised or semi-supervised models, however, because annotated data is hard to obtain. This is where generative models shine. Through the use of latent variables they can be applied in missing data settings. Furthermore they can complete missing entries in partially annotated data sets.

This tutorial is about how to use neural networks inside generative models, thus giving us Deep Generative Models (DGMs). The training method of choice for these models is variational inference (VI). We start out by introducing VI on a basic level. From there we turn to DGMs. We justify them theoretically and give concrete advise on how to implement them. For continuous latent variables, we review the variational autoencoder and use Gaussian reparametrisation to show how to sample latent values from it. We then turn to discrete latent variables for which no reparametrisation exists. Instead, we explain how to use the score-function or REINFORCE gradient estimator in those cases. We finish by explaining how to combine continuous and discrete variables in semi-supervised modelling problems.

2 Schedule

1. Introduction (20 minutes)
   - Maximum likelihood learning
   - Stochastic gradient estimates
   - Unsupervised learning
2. Basics of Variational Inference (45 minutes)
   - Review of posterior inference and intractable marginal likelihoods
   - NLP examples
   - Derivation of variational inference
   - Mean field approximation

20 minutes break

3. DGMs with Continuous Latent Variables (45 minutes)
   - Wake-sleep algorithm
   - Variational autoencoder
   - Gaussian reparametrisation
4. DGMs with Discrete Latent Variables (30 minutes)
   - Latent factor model
   - Why discrete variables cannot be reparametrised
   - Score function gradient estimator
   - Comparison of reparametrisation and score function estimators
   - Semi-supervised learning
5. Q&A

3 About the Presenters

Wilker Aziz is a research associate at the University of Amsterdam (UvA) working on natural language processing problems such as machine translation, textual entailment, and paraphrasing. His research interests include statistical learning, probabilistic models, and methods for approximate inference. Before joining UvA, Wilker worked on exact sampling and optimisation for statistical machine translation at the University of Sheffield (UK) and at the University of Wolverhampton (UK) where he obtained his PhD. Wilker's background is in Computer Engineering which he studied at the Engineering School of the University of São Paulo (Brazil).

Proceedings of the 56th Annual Meeting of the Association for Computational Linguistics-Tutorial Abstracts, pages 8–9
Melbourne, Australia, July 15 - 20, 2018.

Philip Schulz is an applied scientist at Amazon Research. Before joining Amazon, Philip did his PhD at the University of Amsterdam. During the last months of his PhD trajectory, he visited the University of Melbourne. Philip's background is in Linguistics which he studied at the University of Tübingen and UCL in London. These days, his research interests revolve around statistical learning. He has worked on Bayesian graphical models for machine translation. More recently he has extended this line of work towards deep generative models. More broadly, Philip is interested in probabilistic modeling, approximate inference methods and statistical theory.

Connecting Language and Vision to Actions

ACL 2018 Tutorial

Peter Anderson[⋆]
Australian National University
panderson.me
peter.anderson@anu.edu.au

Abhishek Das[†]
Georgia Tech
abhishekdas.com
abhshkdz@gatech.edu

Qi Wu[⋆]
University of Adelaide
qi-wu.me
qi.wu01@adelaide.edu.au

[⋆]Australian Centre for Robotic Vision [†]Machine Learning and Perception Lab

Abstract

A long-term goal of AI research is to build intelligent agents that can *see* the rich visual environment around us, *communicate* this understanding in natural language to humans and other agents, and *act* in a physical or embodied environment. To this end, recent advances at the intersection of language and vision have made incredible progress – from being able to generate natural language descriptions of images/videos, to answering questions about them, to even holding free-form conversations about visual content! However, while these agents can passively describe images or answer (a sequence of) questions about them, they cannot act in the world (what if I cannot answer a question from my current view, or I am asked to move or manipulate something?). Thus, the challenge now is to extend this progress in language and vision to embodied agents that take actions and actively interact with their visual environments.

1 Tutorial Overview

This tutorial will provide an overview of the growing number of multimodal tasks and datasets that combine textual and visual understanding. We will comprehensively review existing state-of-the-art approaches to selected tasks such as image captioning (Chen et al., 2015), visual question answering (VQA) (Antol et al., 2015; Goyal et al., 2017) and visual dialog (Das et al., 2017a,b), presenting the key architectural building blocks (such as co-attention (Lu et al., 2016)) and novel algorithms (such as cooperative/adversarial games (Das et al., 2017b)) used to train models for these tasks. We will then discuss some of the current and upcoming challenges of combining language, vision and actions, and introduce some recently-released interactive 3D simulation environments designed for this purpose (Anderson et al., 2018b; Wu et al., 2018b; Das et al., 2018). The goal of this tutorial is to provide a comprehensive yet accessible overview of existing work and to reduce the entry barrier for new researchers.

In detail, we will first review the building blocks of the neural network architectures used for these tasks, starting from variants of recurrent sequence-to-sequence language models (Ilya Sutskever, 2014), applied to image captioning (Vinyals et al., 2015), optionally with visual attentional mechanisms (Bahdanau et al., 2015; Xu et al., 2015; You et al., 2016; Anderson et al., 2018a). We will then look at evaluation metrics for image captioning (Vedantam et al., 2015; Anderson et al., 2016), before reviewing how these metrics can be optimized directly using reinforcement learning (RL) (Williams, 1992; Rennie et al., 2017).

Next, on the topic of visual question answering, we will look at more sophisticated multimodal attention mechanisms, wherein the network simultaneously attends to visual and textual features (Fukui et al., 2016; Lu et al., 2016). We will see how to combine factual and commonsense reasoning from learnt memory representations (Sukhbaatar et al., 2015) and external knowledge bases (Wang et al., 2016; Wu et al., 2016), and approaches that use the question to dynamically compose the answering neural network from specialized modules (Andreas et al., 2016a,b; Johnson et al., 2017a,b; Hu et al., 2017).

Following the success of adversarial learning in visual recognition (Goodfellow et al., 2014), it has recently been gaining momentum in language modeling (Yu et al., 2016) and in multimodal tasks such as captioning (Dai et al., 2017) and dialog (Wu et al., 2018a). Within visual dia-

Proceedings of the 56th Annual Meeting of the Association for Computational Linguistics-Tutorial Abstracts, pages 10–14
Melbourne, Australia, July 15 - 20, 2018.

log, we will look at recent work that uses cooperative multi-agent tasks as a proxy for training effective visual conversational models via RL (Kottur et al., 2017; Das et al., 2017b).

Finally, as a move away from static datasets, we will cover recent work on building active RL environments for language-vision tasks. Although models that link vision, language and actions have a rich history (Tellex et al., 2011; Paul et al., 2016; Misra et al., 2017), we will focus primarily on embodied 3D environments (Anderson et al., 2018b; Wu et al., 2018b), considering tasks such as visual navigation from natural language instructions (Anderson et al., 2018b), and question answering (Das et al., 2018; Gordon et al., 2018). We will position this work in context of related simulators that also offer significant potential for grounded language learning (Beattie et al., 2016; Zhu et al., 2017). To finish, we will discuss some of the challenges in developing agents for these tasks, as they need to be able to combine active perception, language grounding, commonsense reasoning and appropriate long-term credit assignment to succeed.

2 Structure

The following structure is based on an approximately 3 hour timeframe with a break.

1. Introduction (20 min)
   (a) Language, vision and actions
   (b) Overview of relevant tasks and datasets
      i. Historical progression:
      see → communicate → act
2. Image Captioning (30 min)
   (a) Encoder-decoder for image captioning
   (b) Visual attention mechanisms
      i. Soft and hard visual attention
      ii. Semantic attention
      iii. Bottom-up and top-down attention
   (c) Evaluation
      i. CIDEr metric
      ii. SPICE metric
   (d) Reinforcement learning
      i. Policy gradient optimization
      ii. Self-critical sequence training
3. Visual Question Answering (VQA) (30 min)
   (a) Basic VQA architecture
   (b) Multimodal pooling
      i. Hierarchical co-attention
      ii. Compact bilinear pooling (MCB)
   (c) Dynamic network composition
      i. Neural module networks
      ii. Dynamic memory networks
   (d) Incorporating external knowledge
      i. FVQA
      ii. Ask me anything

——————— BREAK ———————

4. Visual Dialog (20 min)
   (a) Task, datasets and evaluation metrics
   (b) Architectures
      i. Hierarchical RNNs
   (c) Cooperative self-talk
   (d) Adversarial learning
5. Static datasets → Active environments (50 min)
   (a) Interactive 3D datasets and simulators
      i. DeepMind Lab
      ii. AI2-THOR
      iii. SUNCG (House3D / MINOS / HoME)
      iv. Matterport3D (Matterport3D Simulator / MINOS)
   (b) Embodied vision-and-language tasks
      i. Interactive Question Answering
      ii. Embodied Question Answering
      iii. Vision-and-Language Navigation
6. Future directions & conclusion (10 min)

3 Presenters

3.1 Peter Anderson

Peter Anderson is a final year PhD candidate in Computer Science at the Australian National University, supervised by Dr Stephen Gould, and a researcher within the Australian Centre for Robotic Vision (ACRV). His PhD focuses on deep learning for visual understanding in natural language. He was an integral member of the team that won first place in the 2017 Visual Question Answering (VQA) challenge at CVPR, and he has made several contributions in image captioning, including achieving first place on the COCO leaderboard in July 2017. He has published at CVPR, ECCV, EMNLP and ICRA, and spent time at numerous universities and research labs including Adelaide University, Macquarie University, and Microsoft Research. His research is currently focused on vision-and-language understanding in complex 3D environments.

3.2 Abhishek Das

Abhishek Das is a Computer Science PhD student at Georgia Institute of Technology, advised by Dhruv Batra, and working closely with Devi Parikh. He is interested in deep learning and its applications in building agents that can see (computer vision), think (reasoning and interpretability), talk (language modeling) and act (reinforcement learning). He is a recipient of an Adobe Research Fellowship and a Snap Research Fellowship. He has published at CVPR, ICCV, EMNLP, HCOMP and CVIU, co-organized the NIPS 2017 workshop on Visually-Grounded Interaction and Language, and has held visiting positions at Virginia Tech, Queensland Brain Institute and Facebook AI Research. He graduated from Indian Institute of Technology Roorkee in 2015 with a Bachelor's in Electrical Engineering.

3.3 Qi Wu

Dr. Qi Wu, is a research fellow in the Australia Centre for Robotic Vision (ACRV) in the University of Adelaide. Before that, he was a postdoc researcher in the Australia Centre for Visual Technologies (ACVT) in the University of Adelaide. He obtained his PhD degree in 2015 and MSc degree in 2011, in Computer Science from University of Bath, United Kingdom. His research interests are mainly in Computer Vision and Machine Learning. Currently, he is working on the vision-to-language problem and he is especially an expert in the area of Image Captioning and Visual Question Answering (VQA). His attributes-based image captioning model got first place on the COCO Image Captioning Challenge Leader Board in the October of 2015. He has published several papers in prestigious conferences and journals, such as TPAMI, CVPR, ICCV, ECCV, IJCAI and AAAI.

References

Peter Anderson, Basura Fernando, Mark Johnson, and Stephen Gould. 2016. SPICE: Semantic Propositional Image Caption Evaluation. In *ECCV*.

Peter Anderson, Xiaodong He, Chris Buehler, Damien Teney, Mark Johnson, Stephen Gould, and Lei Zhang. 2018a. Bottom-up and top-down attention for image captioning and visual question answering. In *CVPR*.

Peter Anderson, Qi Wu, Damien Teney, Jake Bruce, Mark Johnson, Niko Sünderhauf, Ian Reid, Stephen Gould, and Anton van den Hengel. 2018b. Vision-and-language navigation: Interpreting visually-grounded navigation instructions in real environments. In *CVPR*.

Jacob Andreas, Marcus Rohrbach, Trevor Darrell, and Dan Klein. 2016a. Learning to Compose Neural Networks for Question Answering. In *NAACL-HLT*.

Jacob Andreas, Marcus Rohrbach, Trevor Darrell, and Dan Klein. 2016b. Neural Module Networks. In *CVPR*.

Stanislaw Antol, Aishwarya Agrawal, Jiasen Lu, Margaret Mitchell, Dhruv Batra, C. Lawrence Zitnick, and Devi Parikh. 2015. Vqa: Visual question answering. In *ICCV*.

Dzmitry Bahdanau, Kyunghyun Cho, and Yoshua Bengio. 2015. Neural Machine Translation by Jointly Learning to Align and Translate. In *ICLR*.

Charles Beattie, Joel Z Leibo, Denis Teplyashin, Tom Ward, Marcus Wainwright, Heinrich Küttler, Andrew Lefrancq, Simon Green, Víctor Valdés, Amir Sadik, et al. 2016. Deepmind lab. *arXiv preprint arXiv:1612.03801* .

Xinlei Chen, Tsung-Yi Lin Hao Fang, Ramakrishna Vedantam, Saurabh Gupta, Piotr Dollar, and C. Lawrence Zitnick. 2015. Microsoft COCO Captions: Data Collection and Evaluation Server. *arXiv preprint arXiv:1504.00325* .

Bo Dai, Dahua Lin, Raquel Urtasun, and Sanja Fidler. 2017. Towards diverse and natural image descriptions via a conditional gan. In *ICCV*.

Abhishek Das, Samyak Datta, Georgia Gkioxari, Stefan Lee, Devi Parikh, and Dhruv Batra. 2018. Embodied Question Answering. In *CVPR*.

Abhishek Das, Satwik Kottur, Khushi Gupta, Avi Singh, Deshraj Yadav, José M.F. Moura, Devi Parikh, and Dhruv Batra. 2017a. Visual Dialog. In *CVPR*.

Abhishek Das, Satwik Kottur, José M.F. Moura, Stefan Lee, and Dhruv Batra. 2017b. Learning Cooperative Visual Dialog Agents with Deep Reinforcement Learning. In *ICCV*.

Akira Fukui, Dong Huk Park, Daylen Yang, Anna Rohrbach, Trevor Darrell, and Marcus Rohrbach. 2016. Multimodal compact bilinear pooling for visual question answering and visual grounding. In *EMNLP*.

Ian Goodfellow, Jean Pouget-Abadie, Mehdi Mirza, Bing Xu, David Warde-Farley, Sherjil Ozair, Aaron Courville, and Yoshua Bengio. 2014. Generative adversarial nets. In *NIPS*.

Daniel Gordon, Aniruddha Kembhavi, Mohammad Rastegari, Joseph Redmon, Dieter Fox, and Ali Farhadi. 2018. IQA: Visual question answering in interactive environments. In *CVPR*.

Yash Goyal, Tejas Khot, Douglas Summers-Stay, Dhruv Batra, and Devi Parikh. 2017. Making the V in VQA matter: Elevating the role of image understanding in visual question answering. In *CVPR*.

Ronghang Hu, Jacob Andreas, Marcus Rohrbach, Trevor Darrell, and Kate Saenko. 2017. Learning to reason: End-to-end module networks for visual question answering. In *ICCV*.

Oriol Vinyals Quoc V. Le Ilya Sutskever. 2014. Sequence to Sequence Learning with Neural Networks. In *NIPS*.

Justin Johnson, Bharath Hariharan, Laurens van der Maaten, Li Fei-Fei, C. Lawrence Zitnick, and Ross Girshick. 2017a. CLEVR: A diagnostic dataset for compositional language and elementary visual reasoning. In *CVPR*.

Justin Johnson, Bharath Hariharan, Laurens van der Maaten, Judy Hoffman, Li Fei-Fei, C. Lawrence Zitnick, and Ross Girshick. 2017b. Inferring and executing programs for visual reasoning. In *ICCV*.

Satwik Kottur, José M.F. Moura, Stefan Lee, and Dhruv Batra. 2017. Natural language does not emerge 'naturally' in multi-agent dialog. In *EMNLP*.

Jiasen Lu, Jianwei Yang, Dhruv Batra, and Devi Parikh. 2016. Hierarchical question-image co-attention for visual question answering. In *NIPS*.

Dipendra K Misra, John Langford, and Yoav Artzi. 2017. Mapping instructions and visual observations to actions with reinforcement learning. In *EMNLP*.

Rohan Paul, Jacob Arkin, Nicholas Roy, and Thomas M Howard. 2016. Efficient grounding of abstract spatial concepts for natural language interaction with robot manipulators. In *RSS*.

Steven J Rennie, Etienne Marcheret, Youssef Mroueh, Jarret Ross, and Vaibhava Goel. 2017. Self-critical sequence training for image captioning. In *CVPR*.

Sainbayar Sukhbaatar, Arthur Szlam, Jason Weston, and Rob Fergus. 2015. End-to-end Memory Networks. In *NIPS*.

Stefanie Tellex, Thomas Kollar, Steven Dickerson, Matthew R Walter, Ashis Gopal Banerjee, Seth J Teller, and Nicholas Roy. 2011. Understanding natural language commands for robotic navigation and mobile manipulation. In *AAAI*.

Ramakrishna Vedantam, C. Lawrence Zitnick, and Devi Parikh. 2015. CIDEr: Consensus-Based Image Description Evaluation. In *CVPR*.

Oriol Vinyals, Alexander Toshev, Samy Bengio, and Dumitru Erhan. 2015. Show and tell: A neural image caption generator. In *CVPR*.

Peng Wang, Qi Wu, Chunhua Shen, Anton van den Hengel, and Anthony Dick. 2016. FVQA: Fact-based visual question answering. *TPAMI* .

Ronald J Williams. 1992. Simple statistical gradient-following algorithms for connectionist reinforcement learning. *Machine learning* 8(3-4):229–256.

Qi Wu, Peng Wang, Chunhua Shen, Anthony Dick, and Anton van den Hengel. 2016. Ask Me Anything: Free-form Visual Question Answering Based on Knowledge from External Sources. In *CVPR*.

Qi Wu, Peng Wang, Chunhua Shen, Ian D. Reid, and Anton van den Hengel. 2018a. Are you talking to me? reasoned visual dialog generation through adversarial learning. In *CVPR*.

Yi Wu, Yuxin Wu, Georgia Gkioxari, and Yuandong Tian. 2018b. Building generalizable agents with a realistic and rich 3d environment. *arXiv preprint arXiv:1801.02209* .

Kelvin Xu, Jimmy Ba, Ryan Kiros, Kyunghyun Cho, Aaron C. Courville, Ruslan Salakhutdinov, Richard S. Zemel, and Yoshua Bengio. 2015. Show, Attend and Tell: Neural Image Caption Generation with Visual Attention. In *ICML*.

Quanzeng You, Hailin Jin, Zhaowen Wang, Chen Fang, and Jiebo Luo. 2016. Image captioning with semantic attention. In *CVPR*.

Lantao Yu, Weinan Zhang, Jun Wang, and Yong Yu. 2016. SeqGAN: Sequence generative adversarial nets with policy gradient. In *AAAI*.

Yuke Zhu, Roozbeh Mottaghi, Eric Kolve, Joseph J Lim, Abhinav Gupta, Li Fei-Fei, and Ali Farhadi. 2017. Target-driven visual navigation in indoor scenes using deep reinforcement learning. In *ICRA*.

Beyond Multiword Expressions: Processing Idioms and Metaphors

Valia Kordoni
Humboldt-Universität zu Berlin (Germany)
kordonie@anglistik.hu-berlin.de

1 Introduction

Idioms and metaphors are characteristic to all areas of human activity and to all types of discourse. Their processing is a rapidly growing area in NLP, since they have become a big challenge for NLP systems. Their omnipresence in language has been established in a number of corpus studies and the role they play in human reasoning has also been confirmed in psychological experiments. This makes idioms and metaphors an important research area for computational and cognitive linguistics, and their automatic identification and interpretation indispensable for any semantics-oriented NLP application.

This tutorial aims to provide attendees with a clear notion of the linguistic characteristics of *idioms* and *metaphors*, computational models of *idioms* and *metaphors* using state-of-the-art NLP techniques, their relevance for the intersection of deep learning and natural language processing, what methods and resources are available to support their use, and what more could be done in the future. Our target audience are researchers and practitioners in machine learning, parsing (syntactic and semantic) and language technology, not necessarily experts in *idioms* and *metaphors*, who are interested in tasks that involve or could benefit from considering *idioms* and *metaphors* as a pervasive phenomenon in human language and communication.

This tutorial consists of four parts. Part I starts with an introduction to MWEs and their linguistic dimensions, that is, idiomaticity, syntactic and semantic fixedness, specificity, etc., as well as their statistical characteristics (variability, recurrence, association, etc.). The second half of this part focuses on the specific characteristics of idioms and metaphors (linguistic, conceptual and extended metaphor).

Part II surveys systems for processing idioms and metaphors which incorporate state-of-the-art NLP methods. The second half of this part is dedicated to resources for idioms and metaphors, as well as evaluation.

Part III offers a thorough overview of how and where research on idioms and metaphors can contribute to the intersection of NLP and Deep Learning, particularly focusing on recent advances in the computational treatment of MWEs in the framework of Deep Learning.

Part IV of the tutorial concludes with concrete examples of where idioms and metaphors treatment can contribute to language technology applications such as sentiment analysis, educational applications, dialog systems and digital humanities.

2 Tutorial Outline

1. PART I – General overview:
   (a) Introduction to MWEs: linguistic dimensions (idiomaticity, syntactic and semantic fixedness, specificity, etc.) and statistical dimensions (variability, recurrence, association, etc.)
   (b) Linguistic characteristics of idioms
   (c) Linguistic characteristics of metaphors (linguistic, conceptual and extended metaphor)

2. PART II – Systems for processing idioms and metaphors, resources and evaluation
   (a) Machine learning for idioms and metaphors
   (b) Generation of idioms and metaphors
   (c) Multilingual processing and translation of idioms and metaphors
   (d) Annotation of idioms and metaphors in corpora
   (e) Idioms and metaphors in lexical resources

Proceedings of the 56th Annual Meeting of the Association for Computational Linguistics-Tutorial Abstracts, pages 15–16
Melbourne, Australia, July 15 - 20, 2018.

(f) Evaluation methodologies and frameworks

3. PART III – At the intersection of Deep learning and NLP

   (a) Beyond learning word vectors
   (b) Recursive Neural Networks for parsing idioms and metaphors

4. PART IV – Resources and applications:

   (a) Idioms and metaphors in Language Technology applications: sentiment analysis, educational applications, dialog systems and digital humanities

3 Tutorial Instructor

Valia Kordoni is a professor at Humboldt University Berlin (Deputy Chair for the subject area "English Linguistics"). She is a leader in EU-funded research in Machine Translation, Computational Semantics, and Machine Learning. She has organized conferences and workshops dedicated to research on MWEs, recently including the EACL 2014 *10th Workshop on Multiword Expressions (MWE 2014)* in Gothenburg, Sweden, the NAACL 2015 *11th Workshop on Multiword Expressions* in Denver, Colorado, and the ACL 2016 *12th Workshop on Multiword Expressions* in Berlin, Germany, among others. She has been the Local Chair of *ACL 2016 - The 54th Annual Meeting of the Association for Computational Linguistics* which took place at the Humboldt University Berlin in August 2016. Recent activities of hers include a tutorial on *Robust Automated Natural Language Processing with Multiword Expressions and Collocations* in ACL 2013, as well as a tutorial on *Beyond Words: Deep Learning for Multiword Expressions and Collocations* in ACL 2017. She is the author of *Multiword Expressions - From Linguistic Analysis to Language Technology Applications* (to appear, Springer).

References

Samuel R. Bowman, Christopher Potts, and Christopher D. Manning. 2015a. Learning distributed word representations for natural logic reasoning. In *Proceedings of the AAAI Spring Symposium on Knowledge Representation and Reasoning*.

Samuel R. Bowman, Christopher Potts, and Christopher D. Manning. 2015b. Recursive neural networks can learn logical semantics. In *Proceedings of the 3rd Workshop on Continuous Vector Space Models and their Compositionality*.

Danqi Chen and Christopher Manning. 2014. A fast and accurate dependency parser using neural networks. In *EMNLP*.

Spence Green, Marie-Catherine de Marneffe, and Christopher D. Manning. 2013. Parsing models for identifying multiword expressions. *Computational Linguistics*, 39(1):195–227.

Eric H. Huang, Richard Socher, Christopher D. Manning, and Andrew Y. Ng. 2012. Improving word representations via global context and multiple word prototypes. In *ACL*.

Su Nam Kim and Preslav Nakov. 2011. Large-scale noun compound interpretation using bootstrapping and the web as a corpus. In *EMNLP*, pages 648–658.

Beata Beigman Klebanov, Ekaterina Shutova, and Patricia Lichtenstein, editors. 2014. *Proceedings of the Second Workshop on Metaphor in NLP*. Association for Computational Linguistics, Baltimore, MD, June.

Christopher D. Manning and Hinrich Schütze. 2001. *Foundations of statistical natural language processing*. MIT Press.

Carlos Ramisch, Aline Villavicencio, and Valia Kordoni. to appear. *Special Issue on Multiword Expressions*. ACM TSLP.

Paul Rayson, Scott Songlin Piao, Serge Sharoff, Stefan Evert, and Begoña Villada Moirón. 2010. Multiword expressions: hard going or plain sailing? *Language Resources and Evaluation*, 44(1-2):1–5.

Ivan A. Sag, Timothy Baldwin, Francis Bond, Ann Copestake, and Dan Flickinger. 2001. Multiword expressions: A pain in the neck for nlp. In *In Proc. of the 3rd International Conference on Intelligent Text Processing and Computational Linguistics (CICLing-2002*, pages 1–15.

Violeta Seretan. 2012. *Syntax-Based Collocation Extraction*, volume 44, Text, Speech and Language Technology. Springer.

Ekaterina Shutova, Beata Beigman Klebanov, Joel Tetreault, and Zornitsa Kozareva, editors. 2013a. *Proceedings of the First Workshop on Metaphor in NLP*. Association for Computational Linguistics, Atlanta, Georgia, June.

Ekaterina Shutova, Simone Teufel, and Anna Korhonen. 2013b. Statistical metaphor processing. *Comput. Linguist.*, 39(2):301–353, June.

Aline Villavicencio, Francis Bond, Anna Korhonen, and Diana McCarthy. 2005. Introduction to the special issue on multiword expressions: Having a crack at a hard nut. *Computer Speech & Language*, 19(4):365–377.

Neural Semantic Parsing

Matt Gardner[♠], Pradeep Dasigi[◇], Srinivasan Iyer[♣], Alane Suhr[♡], Luke Zettlemoyer[♣]
[♣]University of Washington, [◇]Carnegie Mellon University,
[♠]Allen Institute for Artificial Intelligence, [♡]Cornell University

1 Introduction

Semantic parsers translate natural language utterances into machine-executable logical forms or programs, and are thus key components in natural language understanding systems. Semantic parsing is a well-established research area, with application in tasks such as question answering, instruction following, voice assistants, and code generation. In the last two years, the models used for semantic parsing have changed dramatically, with the introduction of neural methods that allow us to rethink many of the previous assumptions underlying semantic parsing.

Traditionally, the executable formalisms and models used in semantic parsing research have been heavily reliant on notions of formal semantics in linguistics, such as λ-calculus generated by a CCG parser. However, recent work with neural encoder-decoder semantic parsers allow for more accessible formalisms, such as standard programming languages, and NMT-style models that are much more approachable to a broader NLP audience. We will present an overview of modern neural methods for semantic parsing and how they have changed semantic parsing research.

2 Description

This tutorial will cover how the transition to neural encoder-decoder models has changed semantic parsing research. We aim to both inform those already interested in semantic parsing research of new developments in the field, as well as introduce the topic as an exciting research area to those who are unfamiliar with it.

Current semantic parsing research uses encoder-decoder models that are very similar to machine translation systems. The key difference between these two fields is that semantic parsing translates natural language into a *formal* language, while machine translation translates natural language into a different natural language. The formal language used in semantic parsing research allows for *constrained decoding*, where the model is constrained to only produce outputs that are valid formal statements. We will describe how this is done, and the various approaches researchers have taken to model this constrained decoding.

Encoder-decoder semantic parsing models also allow us to drop our reliance on linguistic formalisms, and much recent work has explored replacing λ-calculus and λ-DCS with standard programming languages like SQL, python, or java. This has the promise of dramatically decreasing annotation costs, allowing researchers to collect much larger and more varied semantic parsing datasets than have previously been available. In our tutorial, we will describe recent efforts in this direction and why programming languages are a natural target for future semantic parsing research.

Neural models also allow representation of continuous, diverse, and less well-defined contexts (e.g., photographs), with methods for representing these contexts that generalize better to new environments (e.g., they don't necessarily require symbolic representations of the environments). The last section of our tutorial will cover recent work on these more complex semantic parsing tasks.

Much of the content covered in this tutorial will have corresponding implementations in the AllenNLP toolkit for NLP research. We will provide a brief overview at the end of the tutorial outlining how to use this toolkit to get started with semantic parsing research.

3 Outline

1. **Introduction**: This section will introduce the theme of the tutorial: how neural encoder-

Proceedings of the 56th Annual Meeting of the Association for Computational Linguistics-Tutorial Abstracts, pages 17–18
Melbourne, Australia, July 15 - 20, 2018. ©2018 Association for Computational Linguistics

decoder models have changed semantic parsing research. We will briefly discuss the complexity of prior systems, and how new models can be seen as very similar to neural machine translation models, with the addition of *constrained decoding*.

2. **Datasets**: Before talking about modern methods, we will spend some time discussing what you can *do* with semantic parsing, and which datasets and tasks are most exciting for current research.

3. **Constrained Decoding**: Current semantic parsing models use an encoder-decoder architecture with constrained decoding. This section will first describe the basic encoder-decoder architecture, then describe how constrained decoding works. There are many ways to parameterize the decoder; we will discuss a simple method in-depth, to give the audience a detailed understanding of the basic model architecture, then describe several other model structures and how they relate to the simple architecture.

   Break

4. **Semantic Parsing as Code Generation**: This section will discuss the choice of formal languages used by semantic parsers, and describe why much recent work has chosen to use standard programming languages instead of more linguistically-motivated representations.

5. **Grounded and Context-Dependent Semantic Parsing**: This section will describe a particularly challenging setting for semantic parsing: where there is additional context or interaction that the parser must take into account when translating natural language to formal language. Neural models provide a natural way to include this context, and we will give an overview of recent work in this direction.

6. **Building Semantic Parsers with AllenNLP**: A brief demonstration of the tools available in the AllenNLP toolkit for doing semantic parsing research.

4 Instructors

Matt Gardner is a research scientist at the Allen Institute for Artificial Intelligence. His research focuses on question answering and semantic parsing. He is the lead maintainer of the AllenNLP toolkit and a host of the NLP Highlights podcast.
Pradeep Dasigi is a PhD student at the Language Technologies Institute in Carnegie Mellon University. His research interest lies in building knowledge-aware language understanding systems, with a recent focus on neural semantic parsing.
Srinivasan Iyer is a graduate student in the Natural Language Processing group at the University of Washington, Seattle. His main research area is context dependent semantic parsing directly from natural language to general purpose programming source code. Other aspects of his research are learning semantic parsers from massive online resources and incorporating user feedback for model improvement.
Alane Suhr is a PhD student in Computer Science at Cornell University. Alane's research interests include developing machine learning methods for understanding natural language grounded in complex environments and interactions. She is a recipient of an NSF Graduate Research Fellowship, the Best Resource Paper award at ACL 2017, and an Outstanding Paper Award at NAACL 2018.
Luke Zettlemoyer Luke Zettlemoyer is an Associate Professor in the Paul G. Allen School of Computer Science & Engineering at the University of Washington. He has a been doing research in semantic parsing for many years, and recently shifted to studying neural models for this problem. Luke's honors include multiple best paper awards, a PECASE award, and an Allen Distinguished Investigator award.

Deep Reinforcement Learning for NLP

William Yang Wang
UC Santa Barbara
william@cs.ucsb.edu

Jiwei Li
Shannon.ai
jiwei_li@shannonai.com

Xiaodong He
JD AI Research
xiaohe@ieee.org

Abstract

Many Natural Language Processing (NLP) tasks (including generation, language grounding, reasoning, information extraction, coreference resolution, and dialog) can be formulated as deep reinforcement learning (DRL) problems. However, since language is often discrete and the space for all sentences is infinite, there are many challenges for formulating reinforcement learning problems of NLP tasks. In this tutorial, we provide a gentle introduction to the foundation of deep reinforcement learning, as well as some practical DRL solutions in NLP. We describe recent advances in designing deep reinforcement learning for NLP, with a special focus on generation, dialogue, and information extraction. We discuss why they succeed, and when they may fail, aiming at providing some practical advice about deep reinforcement learning for solving real-world NLP problems.

1 Tutorial Description

Deep Reinforcement Learning (DRL) (Mnih et al., 2015) is an emerging research area that involves intelligent agents that learn to reason in Markov Decision Processes (MDP). Recently, DRL has achieved many stunning breakthroughs in Atari games (Mnih et al., 2013) and the Go game (Silver et al., 2016). In addition, DRL methods have gained significantly more attentions in NLP in recent years, because many NLP tasks can be formulated as DRL problems that involve incremental decision making. DRL methods could easily combine embedding based representation learning with reasoning, and optimize for a variety of non-differentiable rewards. However, a key challenge for applying deep reinforcement learning techniques to real-world sized NLP problems is the model design issue. This tutorial draws connections from theories of deep reinforcement learning to practical applications in NLP.

In particular, we start with the gentle introduction to the fundamentals of reinforcement learning (Sutton and Barto, 1998; Sutton et al., 2000). We further discuss their modern deep learning extensions such as Deep Q-Networks (Mnih et al., 2015), Policy Networks (Silver et al., 2016), and Deep Hierarchical Reinforcement Learning (Kulkarni et al., 2016). We outline the applications of deep reinforcement learning in NLP, including dialog (Li et al., 2016), semi-supervised text classification (Wu et al., 2018), coreference (Clark and Manning, 2016; Yin et al., 2018), knowledge graph reasoning (Xiong et al., 2017), text games (Narasimhan et al., 2015; He et al., 2016a), social media (He et al., 2016b; Zhou and Wang, 2018), information extraction (Narasimhan et al., 2016; Qin et al., 2018), language and vision (Pasunuru and Bansal, 2017; Misra et al., 2017; Wang et al., 2018a,b,c; Xiong et al., 2018), etc.

We further discuss several critical issues in DRL solutions for NLP tasks, including (1) The efficient and practical design of the action space, state space, and reward functions; (2) The trade-off between exploration and exploitation; and (3) The goal of incorporating linguistic structures in DRL. To address the model design issue, we discuss several recent solutions (He et al., 2016b; Li et al., 2016; Xiong et al., 2017). We then focus on a new case study of hierarchical deep reinforcement learning for video captioning (Wang et al., 2018b), discussing the techniques of leveraging hierarchies in DRL for NLP generation problems. This tutorial aims at introducing deep reinforcement learning methods to researchers in the NLP community. We do not assume any particular prior knowledge in reinforcement learning. The intended length of the tutorial is 3 hours, including a coffee break.

2 Outline

Representation Learning, Reasoning (Learning to Search), and Scalability are three closely related research subjects in Natural Language Processing. In this tutorial, we touch the intersection of all the three research subjects, covering various aspects of the theories of modern deep reinforcement learning methods, and show their successful applications in NLP. This tutorial is organized in three parts:

- **Foundations of Deep Reinforcement Learning.** First, we will provide a brief overview

Proceedings of the 56th Annual Meeting of the Association for Computational Linguistics-Tutorial Abstracts, pages 19–21
Melbourne, Australia, July 15 - 20, 2018.

of reinforcement learning (RL), and discuss the classic settings in RL. We describe classic methods such as Markov Decision Processes, REINFORCE (Williams, 1992), and Q-learning (Watkins, 1989). We introduce model-free and model-based reinforcement learning approaches, and the widely used policy gradient methods. In this part, we also introduce the modern renovation of deep reinforcement learning (Mnih et al., 2015), with a focus on games (Mnih et al., 2013; Silver et al., 2016).

- **Practical Deep Reinforcement Learning: Case Studies in NLP** Second, we will focus on the designing practical DRL models for NLP tasks. In particular, we will take the first deep reinforcement learning solution for dialogue (Li et al., 2016) as a case study. We describe the main contributions of this work: including its design of the reward functions, and why they are necessary for dialog. We then introduce the gigantic action space issue for deep Q-learning in NLP (He et al., 2016a,b), including several solutions. To conclude this part, we discuss interesting applications of DRL in NLP, including information extraction and reasoning.

- **Lessons Learned, Future Directions, and Practical Advices for DRL in NLP** Third, we switch from the theoretical presentations to an interactive demonstration and discussion session: we aim at providing an interactive session to transfer the theories of DRL into practical insights. More specifically, we will discuss three important issues, including problem formulation/model design, exploration vs. exploitation, and the integration of linguistic structures in DRL. We will show case a recent study (Wang et al., 2018b) that leverages hierarchical deep reinforcement learning for language and vision, and extend the discussion. Practical advice including programming advice will be provided as a part of the demonstration.

3 History

The full content of this tutorial has not yet been presented elsewhere, but some parts of this tutorial has also been presented at the following locations in recent years:

1. "*Deep Reinforcement Learning for Knowledge Graph Reasoning*", William Wang, presented at the IBM T. J. Watson Research Center, Yorktown Heights, NY, Bloomberg, New York, NY and Facebook, Menlo Park, CA, total attendance: 150.

2. "*Deep Learning and Continuous Representations for NLP*", Wen-tau Yih, Xiaodong He, and Jianfeng Gao. Tutorial at IJCAI 2016, New York City, total attendance: 100.

3. "*Teaching a Machine to Converse*", Jiwei Li, presented at OSU, UC Berkeley, UCSB, Harbin Inst. of Technology, total attendance: 500.

4 Information About the Presenters

William Wang is an Assistant Professor at the Department of Computer Science, University of California, Santa Barbara. He received his PhD from School of Computer Science, Carnegie Mellon University. He focuses on information extraction and he is the faculty author of DeepPath—the first deep reinforcement learning system for multi-hop reasoning. He has published more than 50 papers at leading conferences and journals including *ACL, EMNLP, NAACL, CVPR, COLING, IJCAI, CIKM, ICWSM, SIGDIAL, IJCNLP, INTERSPEECH, ICASSP, ASRU, SLT, Machine Learning, and Computer Speech & Language*, and he has received paper awards and honors from CIKM, ASRU, and EMNLP. Website: `http://www.cs.ucsb.edu/~william/`

Jiwei Li recently spent three years and received his PhD in Computer Science from Stanford University. His research interests are deep learning and dialogue. He is the most prolific NLP/ML first author during 2012-2016, and the lead author of the first study in deep reinforcement learning for dialogue generation. He is the recipient of a Facebook Fellowship in 2015. Website: `https://web.stanford.edu/~jiweil/`

Xiaodong He is the Deputy Managing Director of JD AI Research and Head of the Deep learning, NLP and Speech Lab, and a Technical Vice President of JD.com. He is also an Affiliate Professor at the University of Washington (Seattle), serves in doctoral supervisory committees. Before joining JD.com, He was with Microsoft for about 15 years, served as Principal Researcher and Research Manager of the DLTC at Microsoft Research, Redmond. His research interests are mainly in artificial intelligence areas including deep learning, natural language, computer vision, speech, information retrieval, and knowledge representation. He has published more than 100 papers in *ACL, EMNLP, NAACL, CVPR, SIGIR, WWW, CIKM, NIPS, ICLR, ICASSP, Proc. IEEE, IEEE TASLP, IEEE SPM*, and other venues. He received several awards including the Outstanding Paper Award at ACL 2015. Website: `http://air.jd.com/people2.html`

References

Kevin Clark and Christopher D Manning. 2016. Deep reinforcement learning for mention-ranking coreference models. *EMNLP*.

Ji He, Jianshu Chen, Xiaodong He, Jianfeng Gao, Lihong Li, Li Deng, and Mari Ostendorf. 2016a. Deep reinforcement learning with a natural language action space. *ACL*.

Ji He, Mari Ostendorf, Xiaodong He, Jianshu Chen, Jianfeng Gao, Lihong Li, and Li Deng. 2016b. Deep reinforcement learning with a combinatorial action space for predicting popular reddit threads. *EMNLP*.

Tejas D Kulkarni, Karthik Narasimhan, Ardavan Saeedi, and Josh Tenenbaum. 2016. Hierarchical deep reinforcement learning: Integrating temporal abstraction and intrinsic motivation. In *NIPS*.

Jiwei Li, Will Monroe, Alan Ritter, Michel Galley, Jianfeng Gao, and Dan Jurafsky. 2016. Deep reinforcement learning for dialogue generation. *EMNLP*.

Dipendra K Misra, John Langford, and Yoav Artzi. 2017. Mapping instructions and visual observations to actions with reinforcement learning. *arXiv preprint arXiv:1704.08795*.

Volodymyr Mnih, Koray Kavukcuoglu, David Silver, Alex Graves, Ioannis Antonoglou, Daan Wierstra, and Martin Riedmiller. 2013. Playing atari with deep reinforcement learning. *arXiv preprint arXiv:1312.5602*.

Volodymyr Mnih, Koray Kavukcuoglu, David Silver, Andrei A Rusu, Joel Veness, Marc G Bellemare, Alex Graves, Martin Riedmiller, Andreas K Fidjeland, Georg Ostrovski, et al. 2015. Human-level control through deep reinforcement learning. *Nature*, 518(7540):529–533.

Karthik Narasimhan, Tejas Kulkarni, and Regina Barzilay. 2015. Language understanding for text-based games using deep reinforcement learning. *EMNLP*.

Karthik Narasimhan, Adam Yala, and Regina Barzilay. 2016. Improving information extraction by acquiring external evidence with reinforcement learning. *EMNLP*.

Ramakanth Pasunuru and Mohit Bansal. 2017. Reinforced video captioning with entailment rewards. *EMNLP*.

Pengda Qin, Weiran Xu, and William Yang Wang. 2018. Robust distant supervision relation extraction via deep reinforcement learning. In *ACL*.

David Silver, Aja Huang, Chris J Maddison, Arthur Guez, Laurent Sifre, George Van Den Driessche, Julian Schrittwieser, Ioannis Antonoglou, Veda Panneershelvam, Marc Lanctot, et al. 2016. Mastering the game of go with deep neural networks and tree search. *Nature*, 529(7587):484–489.

Richard S Sutton and Andrew G Barto. 1998. *Reinforcement learning: An introduction*, volume 1. MIT press Cambridge.

Richard S Sutton, David A McAllester, Satinder P Singh, and Yishay Mansour. 2000. Policy gradient methods for reinforcement learning with function approximation. In *NIPS*.

Xin Wang, Wenhu Chen, Yuan-Fang Wang, and William Yang Wang. 2018a. No metrics are perfect: Adversarial reward learning for visual storytelling. In *ACL*.

Xin Wang, Wenhu Chen, Jiawei Wu, Yuan-Fang Wang, and William Yang Wang. 2018b. Video captioning via hierarchical reinforcement learning. In *CVPR*.

Xin Wang, Wenhan Xiong, Hongmin Wang, and William Yang Wang. 2018c. Look before you leap: Bridging model-free and model-based reinforcement learning for planned-ahead vision-and-language navigation. *arXiv preprint arXiv:1803.07729*.

Christopher John Cornish Hellaby Watkins. 1989. *Learning from delayed rewards*. Ph.D. thesis, King's College, Cambridge.

Ronald J Williams. 1992. Simple statistical gradient-following algorithms for connectionist reinforcement learning. *Machine learning*, 8(3-4):229–256.

Jiawei Wu, Lei Li, and William Yang Wang. 2018. Reinforced co-training. In *NAACL*.

Wenhan Xiong, Xiaoxiao Guo, Mo Yu, Shiyu Chang, and William Yang Wang. 2018. Scheduled policy optimization for natural language communication with intelligent agents. In *IJCAI-ECAI*.

Wenhan Xiong, Thien Hoang, and William Yang Wang. 2017. Deeppath: A reinforcement learning method for knowledge graph reasoning. *EMNLP*.

Qingyu Yin, Yu Zhang, Wei-Nan Zhang, Ting Liu, and William Yang Wang. 2018. Deep reinforcement learning for chinese zero pronoun resolution. In *ACL*.

Xianda Zhou and William Yang Wang. 2018. Mojitalk: Generating emotional responses at scale. In *ACL*.

Multi-lingual Entity Discovery and Linking

Avirup Sil
IBM Research AI
Yorktown Heights, NY
avi@us.ibm.com

Heng Ji
Rensselaer Polytechnic Institute
Troy, NY
jih@rpi.edu

Dan Roth
University of Pennsylvania
Philadelphia, PA
danroth@seas.upenn.edu

Silviu Cucerzan
Microsoft Research
Redmond, WA
silviu@microsoft.com

1 Overall

We live in a golden age of information, where we have access to vast amount of data in various forms: text, video and audio. Over the last few years, one of the key task that has been studied in support of natural language understanding and information extraction from text, is the task of Entity Linking (previously studied as Wikification). Entity Linking (henceforth, EL) (Bunescu and Pasca, 2006; Cucerzan, 2007; Ratinov et al., 2011) is the task of mapping mentions of entities in a text document to an entry in a large catalog of entities such as Wikipedia or another knowledge base (KB). It has also been one of the major tasks in the Knowledge-Base Population track at the Text Analysis Conference (TAC) (McNamee and Dang, 2009b; Ji and Grishman, 2011; Ji et al., 2014). Most works in the literature have used Wikipedia as this target catalog of entities because of its wide coverage and its frequent updates made by the community. The previous Entity Linking tutorial in ACL 2014 (Roth et al., 2014) addressed mostly EL research which have focused on English, the most prevalent language on the web and the one with the largest Wikipedia datasets. However, in the last few years research has shifted to address the EL task in other languages, some of which have very large web presence, such as Spanish (Fahrni et al., 2013; Ji et al., 2014), and Chinese (Cao et al., 2014; Shi et al., 2014) but also in others. In particular, there has been interest in cross-lingual EL (Tsai and Roth, 2016; Sil and Florian, 2016): given a mention in a foreign language document, map it to the corresponding page in the English Wikipedia. Beyond the motivation that drives the English EL task – knowledge acquisition and information extraction – in the cross-lingual case and especially when dealing with low resource languages, the hope is to provide improved natural language understanding capabilities for the many languages for which we have few linguistic resources and annotation and no machine translation technology. The LoreHLT2016-2017 evaluation[1] and TAC 2017 pilot evaluation [2] target really low-resource languages like Northern Sotho or Kikuyu which only have about 4000 Wikipedia pages (about 1/1000 the size of the English wikipedia).

The primary goals of this tutorial are to review the framework of cross-lingual EL and motivate it as a broad paradigm for the Information Extraction task. We will start by discussing the traditional EL techniques and metrics and address questions relevant to the adequacy of these to across domains and languages. We will then present more recent approaches such as Neural EL, discuss the basic building blocks of a state-of-the-art neural EL system and analyze some of the current results on English EL. We will then proceed to Cross-lingual EL and discuss methods that work across languages. In particular, we will discuss and compare multiple methods that make use of multi-lingual word embeddings. We will also present EL methods that work for both name tagging and linking in very low resource languages. Finally, we will discuss the uses of cross-lingual EL in a variety of applications like search engines and commercial product selling applications. Also, contrary to the 2014 EL tutorial, we will also focus on Entity Discovery which is an essential component of EL.

The tutorial will be useful for both senior and junior researchers (in academia and industry) with interests in cross-source information extraction and linking, knowledge acquisition, and the use of acquired knowledge in natural language processing and information extraction. We will try to provide a concise road-map of recent approaches, perspectives, and results, as well as point to some of our EL resources that are available to the research community.

[1] https://lorehlt.nist.gov/

[2] http://nlp.cs.rpi.edu/kbp/2017/taskspec_pilot.pdf

Proceedings of the 56th Annual Meeting of the Association for Computational Linguistics-Tutorial Abstracts, pages 22–29
Melbourne, Australia, July 15 - 20, 2018.

2 Brief Tutorial Outline

2.1 Motivation and Overview [20 mins]

We will motivate the general EL problem (for English) by teaching the general methods that incorporate distance measures (Ratinov et al., 2011; Sil and Yates, 2013; Cheng and Roth, 2013). We will then briefly discuss multi-lingual IE problems and motivate cross-lingual EL (Ji et al., 2014; Sil and Florian, 2016). Then we will motivate the new trend of modeling distributional representations instead of distance.

2.2 Key Challenges and Multi-lingual Embeddings [20 mins]

We will present some key challenges daunting high-performing *traditional* EL systems and candidate generation and transliteration (Tsai and Roth, 2018) from a knowledge-base. We will also present the models for *traditional* cross-lingual EL (Sil and Florian, 2016; Tsai and Roth, 2016) and discuss some of their challenges: matching context between non-English documents with the English Wikipedia. Recently, neural Entity Discovery and Linking (henceforth, EDL) techniques have combated some of these challenges. These systems use multi-lingual embeddings which are essential building blocks for these neural architectures. Hence, before diving into the architectures we will survey multi-lingual embedding techniques (Mikolov et al., 2013c; Faruqui and Dyer, 2014; Ammar et al., 2016) and which ones work best for neural EL systems and motivate neural EL.

2.3 Neural Methods for EDL [30 mins]

Various shared tasks such as TAC-KBP, ACE and CONLL, along with corpora like OntoNotes and ERE have provided the community substantial amount of annotations for both entity mention extraction (1,500+ documents) and entity linking (5,000+ query entities). Therefore supervised models have become popular again for each step of EDL. Among all of the supervised learning frameworks for mention extraction, the most popular one is a combined Deep Neural Networks architecture consisted of Bi-directional Long Short-Term Memory networks (Bi-LSTM) (Graves et al., 2013) and CRFs (Lample et al., 2016). In TAC-KBP2017 many teams trained this framework from the same training data (KBP2015 and KBP2016 EDL corpora) and the same set of features (word and entity embeddings), but got very different results. The mention extraction F-score gap between the best system and the worst system is about 24%. We will provide a systematic comparison and analysis on reasons that cause this big gap. We will also introduce techniques to make the framework more robust to noise in low-resource settings.

We will then teach neural EL architectures (Globerson et al., 2016; Gupta et al., 2017a; Sil et al., 2018) that can tackle some of the challenges of the traditional systems. Then we will proceed to cross-lingual neural EL and survey the pipelines that most of these EL systems employ: cross-lingual NER and in-document coreference resolution. We will talk about how to model the contexts using various neural techniques like CNNs, LSTMs etc. and how systems compute similarity metrics of varying granularity (Francis-Landau et al., 2016; Sil et al., 2018).

2.4 Coffee break: [30 minutes]

2.5 Language Universal Methods for Cross-lingual EDL [30 mins]

We will then present some recent advances at developing low-cost approaches to perform cross-lingual EL for 282 Wikipedia languages, such as deriving silver-standard annotations by transferring annotations from English to other languages through cross-lingual links and KB properties, refining annotations through self-training and topic selection, deriving language-specific morphology features from anchor links, and mining word translation pairs from cross-lingual links (Pan et al., 2017a). We will also introduce some recent extensions along this line of work, including extending the number of entity types from five to thousands, and its impact on other NLP applications such as Machine Translation.

2.6 Multiple Knowledge Bases [25 mins]

A task that is similar to multi-lingual EL in both definition and approaches is domain-specific linking of entities in documents based on a given set of domains/corresponding knowledge repositories (Gao and Cucerzan, 2017). This task is important for applications such as the analysis and indexing of corporate document repositories, in which many of the entities of interest are not part of the general-knowledge but are rather company-specific and may need to be kept private. Conflating such terminologies and knowledge into one single knowledge model would be both daunting and undesirable. Thus, similarly to handling multiple languages, a system built for multiple-domain linking, has to model each domain separately. We will discuss a multi-KB entity linking framework that employs one general-knowledge KB and a large set of domain-specific KBs as linking targets that extends the work from (Cucerzan, 2007, 2014a), as well as a supervised model with a large and diverse set of features to detect when a domain-specific KB matches a document targeted for entity analysis (Gao and Cucerzan, 2017).

2.7 New Tasks, Trends and Open Questions [15 mins]

Here, we will address some of the new settings: multi-lingual EL for search engines (Pappu et al., 2017; Tan et al., 2017). We will discuss some open questions such as improving the title candidate generation process for situations where the corresponding titles only exist in the English Wikipedia and also investigate the topological structure of related languages and exploit cross-lingual knowledge transfer to enhance the quality of extraction and linking (Tsai and Roth, 2018). We will also discuss EL for noisy data like social media (Meij et al., 2012; Guo et al., 2013). Finally, we will discuss the possibilities of extending the ideas taught in this EL tutorial to other multi-lingual IE tasks.

2.8 System Demos and Resources [10 mins]

Finally, we will show some demos of multi-lingual EL systems from the industry and academia. We will also provide pointers to resources, including data sets and software.

3 Tutorial Instructors

- **Name:** Avirup Sil
  Affiliation: IBM Research AI
  Email: avi@us.ibm.com
  Website: Avi's Webpage
  Avi is a Research Staff Member and the chair of the NLP community at IBM Research AI. His research interests are in multi-lingual information extraction from large text collection (cross-lingual entity extraction, disambiguation and slot filling), machine learning and knowledge representation. Avi has published several papers on Entity Linking and his systems at IBM have obtained top scores in TAC-KBP annual multi-lingual entity linking evaluations. Avi is an area chair for Information Extraction at NAACL 2018 and also for COLING 2018. He is also organizing the workshop on the "Relevance of Linguistic Structure in Neural NLP" at ACL 2018.

- **Name:** Heng Ji
  Affiliation: Rensselaer Polytechnic Institute
  Email: jih@rpi.edu
  Website: Heng's Webpage
  Heng Ji is the Edward G. Hamilton Development Chair Professor in Computer Science Department of Rensselaer Polytechnic Institute. Her research interests focus on Natural Language Processing, especially on Cross-source Information Extraction and Knowledge Base Population. She coordinated the NIST TAC Knowledge Base Population task since 2010 and has published many papers on entity discovery and linking. Heng has co-taught the "Wikification and Beyond: The Challenges of Entity and Concept Grounding" tutorial with Dan Roth at ACL 2014.

- **Name:** Dan Roth
  Affiliation: University of Pennsylvania
  Email: danroth@seas.upenn.edu
  Website: Dan's Webpage
  Dan Roth is the Eduardo D. Glandt Distinguished Professor at the Department of Computer and Information Science, University of Pennsylvania. He is a fellow of AAAS, AAAI, ACL, and the ACM and the winner of the IJCAI-2017 John McCarthy Award, for "major conceptual and theoretical advances in the modeling of natural language understanding, machine learning, and reasoning." Roth has published broadly in machine learning, natural language processing, knowledge representation and reasoning, and has developed several machine learning based natural language processing systems that are widely used in the computational linguistics community and in industry. Over the last few years he has worked on Entity Linking and Wikification. He has taught several tutorials at ACL/NAACL/ECL and other forums. Dan has co-taught the "Wikification and Beyond: The Challenges of Entity and Concept Grounding" tutorial with Heng Ji at ACL 2014.

- **Name:** Silviu Cucerzan
  Affiliation: Microsoft Research
  Email: silviu@microsoft.com
  Website: Silviu's Webpage
  Silviu Cucerzan is a Principal Researcher at Microsoft Research and the Bing Knowledge Graph group. His research has focused on topics at the intersection of NLP

and IR with concrete applications to industry, including multilingual spelling correction, question answering, entity recognition and linking, query suggestion, vertical search, and ads selection. Many of the technologies developed by Silviu have been shipped with Microsoft products. The NEMO entity linking system developed by Silviu has scored the top performance during the four consecutive years it participated in the TAC-KBP evaluations organized by NIST and LDC.

References

Waleed Ammar, George Mulcaire, Yulia Tsvetkov, Guillaume Lample, Chris Dyer, and Noah A Smith. 2016. Massively multilingual word embeddings. *arXiv preprint arXiv:1602.01925* .

Ivo Anastácio, Bruno Martins, Pável Calado, et al. 2011. Supervised learning for linking named entities to knowledge base entries.

Roi Blanco, Giuseppe Ottaviano, and Edgar Meij. 2015. Fast and space-efficient entity linking for queries. In *Proceedings of the Eighth ACM International Conference on Web Search and Data Mining*. ACM, pages 179–188.

Antoine Bordes, Jason Weston, Ronan Collobert, and Yoshua Bengio. 2011. Learning structured embeddings of knowledge bases. In *Conference on Artificial Intelligence*. EPFL-CONF-192344.

R. Bunescu and M. Pasca. 2006. Using encyclopedic knowledge for named entity disambiguation. In *EACL*.

Ziqiang Cao, Sujian Li, and Heng Ji. 2014. Joint learning of chinese words, terms and keywords. In *EMNLP*.

David Carmel, Ming-Wei Chang, Evgeniy Gabrilovich, Bo-June Paul Hsu, and Kuansan Wang. 2014. Erd'14: entity recognition and disambiguation challenge. In *Proceedings of the 37th international ACM SIGIR conference on Research & development in information retrieval*.

Jianpeng Cheng, Li Dong, and Mirella Lapata. 2016. Long short-term memory-networks for machine reading. *CoRR* abs/1601.06733. `http://arxiv.org/abs/1601.06733`.

X. Cheng and D. Roth. 2013. Relational inference for wikification. In *Proc. of the Conference on Empirical Methods in Natural Language Processing (EMNLP)*.

Andrew Chisholm and Ben Hachey. 2015. Entity disambiguation with web links. *Transactions of the Association for Computational Linguistics* 3:145–156.

S. Cucerzan. 2014a. Named entities made obvious: The participation in the erd 2014 evaluation. In *SIGIR Forum 2014*.

Silviu Cucerzan. 2007. Large-scale named entity disambiguation based on wikipedia data. In *EMNLP-CoNLL*. pages 708–716.

Silviu Cucerzan. 2014b. The MSR System for Entity Linking at TAC 2014. In *Text Analysis Conference*.

Silviu Cucerzan and Avirup Sil. 2013. The MSR Systems for Entity Linking and Temporal Slot Filling at TAC 2013. In *Text Analysis Conference*.

Hong-Jie Dai, Richard Tzong-Han Tsai, Wen-Lian Hsu, et al. 2011. Entity disambiguation using a markov-logic network. In *IJCNLP*.

Nilesh N. Dalvi, Ravi Kumar, and Bo Pang. 2012. Object matching in tweets with spatial models. In *WSDM*. pages 43–52.

Alexandre Davis, Adriano Veloso, Altigran S da Silva, Wagner Meira Jr, and Alberto HF Laender. 2012. Named entity disambiguation in streaming data. In *ACL*.

Gianluca Demartini, Djellel Eddine Difallah, and Philippe Cudré-Mauroux. 2012. Zencrowd: leveraging probabilistic reasoning and crowdsourcing techniques for large-scale entity linking. In *Proceedings of the 21st international conference on World Wide Web*.

Li Dong, Furu Wei, Ming Zhou, and Ke Xu. 2015. Question answering over freebase with multicolumn convolutional neural networks. In *Proceedings of the 53rd Annual Meeting of the Association for Computational Linguistics and the 7th International Joint Conference on Natural Language Processing*. volume 1, pages 260–269.

Greg Durrett and Dan Klein. 2014. A joint model for entity analysis: Coreference, typing, and linking. In *Transactions of the Association for Computational Linguistics*.

Angela Fahrni, Benjamin Heinzerling, Thierry Göckel, and Michael Strube. 2013. Hits monolingual and cross-lingual entity linking system at TAC 2013. In *Text Analysis Conference*.

Manaal Faruqui and Chris Dyer. 2014. Improving vector space word representations using multilingual correlation. ACL.

Matthew Francis-Landau, Greg Durrett, and Dan Klein. 2016. Capturing semantic similarity for entity linking with convolutional neural networks. In *Proc. NAACL 2016*.

Octavian-Eugen Ganea, Marina Ganea, Aurelien Lucchi, Carsten Eickhoff, and Thomas Hofmann. 2016. Probabilistic bag-of-hyperlinks model for entity linking. In *Proceedings of the 25th International*

Conference on World Wide Web. International World Wide Web Conferences Steering Committee, pages 927–938.

N. Gao and S. Cucerzan. 2017. Entity linking to one thousand knowledge bases. In *ECIR 2017*.

Felix A Gers, Jürgen Schmidhuber, and Fred Cummins. 2000. Learning to forget: Continual prediction with lstm. *Neural computation* 12(10):2451–2471.

Amir Globerson, Nevena Lazic, Soumen Chakrabarti, Amarnag Subramanya, Michael Ringgaard, and Fernando Pereira. 2016. Collective entity resolution with multi-focal attention. *ACL* .

Alan Graves, Navdeep Jaitly, and Abdel-rahman Mohamed. 2013. Hybrid speech recognition with deep bidirectional lstm. In *Automatic Speech Recognition and Understanding, 2013 IEEE Workshop on*.

Stephen Guo, Ming-Wei Chang, and Emre Kıcıman. 2013. To link or not to link? a study on end-to-end tweet entity linking. In *NAACL*.

Zhaochen Guo and Denilson Barbosa. 2014. Robust entity linking via random walks. In *Proceedings of the 23rd ACM International Conference on Conference on Information and Knowledge Management*. ACM, pages 499–508.

Nitish Gupta, Sameer Singh, and Dan Roth. 2017a. Entity linking via joint encoding of types, descriptions, and context. In *Proceedings of the 2017 Conference on Empirical Methods in Natural Language Processing*. pages 2671–2680.

Nitish Gupta, Sameer Singh, and Dan Roth. 2017b. Entity linking via joint encoding of types, descriptions, and context. In *EMNLP*. `http://cogcomp.org/papers/GuptaSiRo17.pdf`.

Ben Hachey, Will Radford, and James R. Curran. 2011. Graph-based named entity linking with wikipedia. In *The 12th International Conference on Web Information System Engineering (WISE)*.

X. Han, L. Sun, and J. Zhao. 2011a. Collective entity linking in web text: a graph-based method. In *SIGIR*.

Xianpei Han, Le Sun, and Jun Zhao. 2011b. Collective entity linking in web text: a graph-based method. In *Proceedings of the 34th international ACM SIGIR conference on Research and development in Information Retrieval*. ACM, pages 765–774.

Zhengyan He, Shujie Liu, Mu Li, Ming Zhou, Longkai Zhang, and Houfeng Wang. 2013. Learning entity representation for entity disambiguation. In *ACL (2)*. pages 30–34.

Sepp Hochreiter and Jürgen Schmidhuber. 1997. Long short-term memory. *Neural computation* 9(8):1735–1780.

Johannes Hoffart, Fabian M Suchanek, Klaus Berberich, and Gerhard Weikum. 2013. Yago2: A spatially and temporally enhanced knowledge base from wikipedia. *Artificial Intelligence* 194:28–61.

Neil Houlsby and Massimiliano Ciaramita. 2014. A scalable gibbs sampler for probabilistic entity linking. In *Advances in Information Retrieval*, Springer, pages 335–346.

Zhiting Hu, Poyao Huang, Yuntian Deng, Yingkai Gao, and Eric P Xing. 2015. Entity hierarchy embedding. In *Proceedings of the 53rd Annual Meeting of the Association for Computational Linguistics and the 7th International Joint Conference on Natural Language Processing (ACL-IJCNLP)*. volume 1, pages 1292–1300.

Hongzhao Huang, Larry Heck, and Heng Ji. 2015. Leveraging deep neural networks and knowledge graphs for entity disambiguation. *arXiv preprint arXiv:1504.07678* .

Mohit Iyyer, Varun Manjunatha, Jordan Boyd-Graber, and Hal Daumé III. 2015. Deep unordered composition rivals syntactic methods for text classification. In *Proceedings of the 53rd Annual Meeting of the Association for Computational Linguistics and the 7th International Joint Conference on Natural Language Processing*. volume 1, pages 1681–1691.

Heng Ji, HT Dang, J Nothman, and B Hachey. 2014. Overview of tac-kbp2014 entity discovery and linking tasks. In *Proc. Text Analysis Conference (TAC2014)*.

Heng Ji and Ralph Grishman. 2011. Knowledge base population: Successful approaches and challenges. In *Proceedings of ACL2011*.

Heng Ji, Ralph Grishman, and Hoa Trang Dang. 2011. Overview of the tac2011 knowledge base population track. *TAC* .

Heng Ji, Joel Nothman, Ben Hachey, and Radu Florian. 2015. Overview of tac-kbp2015 tri-lingual entity discovery and linking. In *TAC*.

Alex Judea, Benjamin Heinzerling, Angela Fahrni, and Michael Strube. 2014. Hits monolingual and cross-lingual entity linking system at TAC 2014. In *Text Analysis Conference*.

Nal Kalchbrenner, Edward Grefenstette, and Phil Blunsom. 2014. A convolutional neural network for modelling sentences. *arXiv preprint arXiv:1404.2188* .

Yoon Kim. 2014. Convolutional neural networks for sentence classification. *arXiv preprint arXiv:1408.5882* .

Guillaume Lample, Miguel Ballesteros, Kazuya Kawakami, Sandeep Subramanian, and Chris Dyer. 2016. Neural architectures for named entity recognition. In *Proceeddings of the 2016 Conference of the North American Chapter of the Association for Computational Linguistics Human Language Technologies*.

Nevena Lazic, Amarnag Subramanya, Michael Ringgaard, and Fernando Pereira. 2015. Plato: A selective context model for entity resolution. *Transactions of the Association for Computational Linguistics* 3:503–515.

Hailun Lin, Zeya Zhao, Yantao Jia, Yuanzhuo Wang, Jinhua Xiong, Xiaojing Li, Yuxiao Chang, Manling Li, Hongbo Xu, and Xueqi Cheng. 2014. Openkn at tac kbp 2014. In *Text Analysis Conference*.

T. Lin, P. Pantel, M. Gamon, A. Kannan, and A. Fuxman. 2012a. Active objects: actions for entity-centric search. In *Proceedings of the 21st international conference on World Wide Web*. pages 589–598.

Thomas Lin, Mausam, and Oren Etzioni. 2012b. Entity Linking at Web Scale. In *AKBC-WEKEX*.

Thomas Lin, Mausam, and Oren Etzioni. 2012c. No Noun Phrase Left Behind: Detecting and Typing Unlinkable Entities. In *EMNLP*.

Yankai Lin, Zhiyuan Liu, Maosong Sun, Yang Liu, and Xuan Zhu. 2015. Learning entity and relation embeddings for knowledge graph completion. In *AAAI*. pages 2181–2187.

Ying Lin, Chin-Yew Lin, and Heng Ji. 2017. List-only entity linking. In *Proceedings of the 55th Annual Meeting of the Association for Computational Linguistics (Volume 2: Short Papers)*. volume 2, pages 536–541.

Dan Liu, Wei Lin, Shiliang Zhang, Si Wei, and Hui Jiang. 2016. Neural networks models for entity discovery and linking. *arXiv preprint arXiv:1611.03558* .

Xiaoqiang Luo, Radu Florian, and Todd Ward. 2009. Improving coreference resolution by using conversational metadata. In *NAACL*. Association for Computational Linguistics, pages 201–204.

Xiaoqiang Luo, Abe Ittycheriah, Hongyan Jing, Nanda Kambhatla, and Salim Roukos. 2004. A mention-synchronous coreference resolution algorithm based on the bell tree. In *ACL*. page 135.

James Mayfield. 2013. Overview of the kbp 2013 entity linking track.

P. McNamee and H. T Dang. 2009a. Overview of the TAC 2009 Knowledge Base Population Track. In *Text Analysis Conference*.

Paul McNamee and Hoa Trang Dang. 2009b. Knowledge base population: Successful approaches and challenges. In *Proceedings of TAC2009*.

Paul McNamee, Mark Dredze, Adam Gerber, Nikesh Garera, Tim Finin, James Mayfield, Christine Piatko, Delip Rao, David Yarowsky, and Markus Dreyer. 2009. HLTCOE Approaches to Knowledge Base Population at TAC 2009. In *Text Analysis Conference*.

Paul McNamee, James Mayfield, Douglas W Oard, Tan Xu, Ke Wu, Veselin Stoyanov, and David Doermann. 2011. Cross-language entity linking in maryland during a hurricane.

Edgar Meij, Wouter Weerkamp, and Maarten de Rijke. 2012. Adding semantics to microblog posts. In *WSDM*.

Pablo N. Mendes, Max Jakob, and Christian Bizer. 2011. Evaluating DBpedia Spotlight for the TAC-KBP Entity Linking Task. In *TAC*.

Yuval Merhav, Joel Barry, James Clarke, David Murgatroyd, and One Alewife Center. 2013. Basis technology at tac 2013 entity linking .

Qingliang Miao, Ruiyu Fang, Yao Meng, and Shu Zhang. 2013. Frdc's cross-lingual entity linking system at tac 2013.

Rada Mihalcea and Andras Csomai. 2007. Wikify!: Linking documents to encyclopedic knowledge. In *CIKM*. pages 233–242.

Tomas Mikolov, Kai Chen, Greg Corrado, and Jeffrey Dean. 2013a. Efficient estimation of word representations in vector space. *arXiv preprint arXiv:1301.3781* .

Tomas Mikolov, Quoc V Le, and Ilya Sutskever. 2013b. Exploiting similarities among languages for machine translation. *arXiv preprint arXiv:1309.4168* .

Tomas Mikolov, Ilya Sutskever, Kai Chen, Greg S Corrado, and Jeff Dean. 2013c. Distributed representations of words and phrases and their compositionality. In *NIPS*. pages 3111–3119.

Sean Monahan, Dean Carpenter, Maxim Gorelkin, Kevin Crosby, and Mary Brunson. 2014. Populating a knowledge base with entities and events. In *Text Analysis Conference*.

Thien Huu Nguyen, Yifan He, Maria Pershina, Xiang Li, and Ralph Grishman. 2014. New york university 2014 knowledge base population systems. In *Text Analysis Conference*.

Mark Palatucci, Dean Pomerleau, Geoffrey E Hinton, and Tom M Mitchell. 2009. Zero-shot learning with semantic output codes. In *Advances in neural information processing systems*. pages 1410–1418.

Xiaoman Pan, Boliang Zhang, Jonathan May, Joel Nothman, Kevin Knight, and Heng Ji. 2017a. Cross-lingual name tagging and linking for 282 languages. In *Proc. the 55th Annual Meeting of the Association for Computational Linguistics (ACL2017)*.

Xiaoman Pan, Boliang Zhang, Jonathan May, Joel Nothman, Kevin Knight, and Heng Ji. 2017b. Cross-lingual name tagging and linking for 282 languages. In *Proceedings of the 55th Annual Meeting of the Association for Computational Linguistics (Volume 1: Long Papers)*. volume 1, pages 1946–1958.

Aasish Pappu, Roi Blanco, Yashar Mehdad, Amanda Stent, and Kapil Thadani. 2017. Lightweight multilingual entity extraction and linking. In *Proceedings of the Tenth ACM International Conference on Web Search and Data Mining*. ACM, pages 365–374.

Maria Pershina, Yifan He, and Ralph Grishman. 2015. Personalized page rank for named entity disambiguation. In *HLT-NAACL*. pages 238–243.

Xuan-Hieu Phan, Le-Minh Nguyen, and Susumu Horiguchi. 2008. Learning to classify short and sparse text & web with hidden topics from large-scale data collections. In *Proceedings of the 17th international conference on World Wide Web*.

L. Ratinov, D. Roth, D. Downey, and M. Anderson. 2011. Local and global algorithms for disambiguation to wikipedia. In *ACL*. http://cogcomp.cs.illinois.edu/papers/RRDA11.pdf.

Dan Roth, Heng Ji, Ming-Wei Chang, and Taylor Cassidy. 2014. Wikification and beyond: The challenges of entity and concept grounding. In *ACL Tutorials*.

Yelong Shen, Xiaodong He, Jianfeng Gao, Li Deng, and Grégoire Mesnil. 2014. Learning semantic representations using convolutional neural networks for web search. In *Proceedings of the companion publication of the 23rd international conference on World wide web companion*. International World Wide Web Conferences Steering Committee, pages 373–374.

Xing Shi, Kevin Knight, and Heng Ji. 2014. How to speak a language without knowing it. In *ACL*.

Avirup Sil. 2013. Exploring Re-ranking Approaches for Joint Named-Entity Recognition and Linking. In *ACM PIKM*.

Avirup Sil, Ernest Cronin, Penghai Nie, Yinfei Yang, Ana-Maria Popescu, and Alexander Yates. 2012. Linking Named Entities to Any Database. In *EMNLP-CoNLL*.

Avirup Sil, Georgiana Dinu, and Radu Florian. 2015. The ibm systems for trilingual entity discovery and linking at tac 2015. In *Proceedings of the Eighth Text Analysis Conference (TAC2015)*.

Avirup Sil and Radu Florian. 2016. One for all: Towards language independent named entity linking. *ACL* .

Avirup Sil, Gourab Kundu, Radu Florian, and Wael Hamza. 2018. Neural cross-lingual entity linking. In *Proc. Association for the Advancement of Artificial Intelligence (AAAI)*.

Avirup Sil and Alexander Yates. 2013. Re-ranking for Joint Named-Entity Recognition and Linking. In *CIKM*.

Sameer Singh, Amarnag Subramanya, Fernando Pereira, and Andrew McCallum. 2012. Wikilinks: A large-scale cross-document coreference corpus labeled via links to wikipedia. *University of Massachusetts, Amherst, Tech. Rep. UM-CS-2012-015* .

Richard Socher, Danqi Chen, Christopher D Manning, and Andrew Ng. 2013a. Reasoning with neural tensor networks for knowledge base completion. In *Advances in Neural Information Processing Systems*. pages 926–934.

Richard Socher, Milind Ganjoo, Christopher D Manning, and Andrew Ng. 2013b. Zero-shot learning through cross-modal transfer. In *Advances in neural information processing systems*. pages 935–943.

Richard Socher, Brody Huval, Christopher D Manning, and Andrew Y Ng. 2012. Semantic compositionality through recursive matrix-vector spaces. In *EMNLP*. pages 1201–1211.

Richard Socher, Alex Perelygin, Jean Y Wu, Jason Chuang, Christopher D Manning, Andrew Y Ng, and Christopher Potts. 2013c. Recursive deep models for semantic compositionality over a sentiment treebank. In *EMNLP*. volume 1631, page 1642.

Valentin I Spitkovsky and Angel X Chang. 2012. A cross-lingual dictionary for english wikipedia concepts. In *LREC*. pages 3168–3175.

Yaming Sun, Lei Lin, Duyu Tang, Nan Yang, Zhenzhou Ji, and Xiaolong Wang. 2015. Modeling mention, context and entity with neural networks for entity disambiguation. In *IJCAI*. pages 1333–1339.

Martin Sundermeyer, Ralf Schlüter, and Hermann Ney. 2012. Lstm neural networks for language modeling. In *INTERSPEECH*. pages 194–197.

Ilya Sutskever, Oriol Vinyals, and Quoc V Le. 2014. Sequence to sequence learning with neural networks. In *Advances in neural information processing systems*. pages 3104–3112.

Chuanqi Tan, Furu Wei, Pengjie Ren, Weifeng Lv, and Ming Zhou. 2017. Entity linking for queries by searching wikipedia sentences. *arXiv preprint arXiv:1704.02788* .

Chen-Tse Tsai and Dan Roth. 2016. Cross-lingual wikification using multilingual embeddings. In *Proceedings of NAACL-HLT*. pages 589–598.

Chen-Tse Tsai and Dan Roth. 2018. Learning better name translation for cross-lingual wikification. In *Proceedings of The Conference on Artificial Intelligence (AAAI)*. http://cogcomp.org/papers/2018_aaai_semanticilp.pdf.

Chi Wang, Kaushik Chakrabarti, Tao Cheng, and Surajit Chaudhuri. 2012. Targeted disambiguation of ad-hoc, homogeneous sets of named entities. In *Proceedings of the 21st international conference on World Wide Web*.

Han Wang, Jin Guang Zheng, Xiaogang Ma, Peter Fox, and Heng Ji. 2015. Language and domain independent entity linking with quantified collective validation. In *Proc. Conference on Empirical Methods in Natural Language Processing (EMNLP2015)*.

Zhen Wang, Jianwen Zhang, Jianlin Feng, and Zheng Chen. 2014. Knowledge graph and text jointly embedding. In *EMNLP*. Citeseer, pages 1591–1601.

Zhiguo Wang, Haitao Mi, Wael Hamza, and Radu Florian. 2016a. Multi-perspective context matching for machine comprehension. *arXiv preprint arXiv:1612.04211* .

Zhiguo Wang, Haitao Mi, and Abraham Ittycheriah. 2016b. Sentence similarity learning by lexical decomposition and composition. *COLING* .

Daniel S. Weld, Raphael Hoffmann, and Fei Wu. 2009. Using Wikipedia to Bootstrap Open Information Extraction. In *ACM SIGMOD Record*.

UK WR143PS. 1989. Training stochastic model recognition algorithms as networks can lead to maximum mutual information estimation of parameters .

Ikuya Yamada, Hiroyuki Shindo, Hideaki Takeda, and Yoshiyasu Takefuji. 2016. Joint learning of the embedding of words and entities for named entity disambiguation. *arXiv:1601.01343* .

Z. Zheng, X. Si, F. Li, E. Chang, and X. Zhu. 2012. Entity disambiguation with freebase. In *Proceedings of the 2012 IEEE/WIC/ACM International Conference on Web Intelligence (WI'2012)*.

Author Index

Association for Computational Linguistics
209 N. Eighth Street
Stroudsburg, Pennsylvania 18360

ISBN 978-1-5108-6709-3

CURRAN ASSOCIATES INC.
proceedings.com